MORE INDIAN ERNIE:
INSIGHTS FROM THE STREETS

T0345209

Purich Publishing, an imprint of UBC Press
2029 West Mall
Vancouver, BC; Canada V6T 1Z2
www.ubcpress.ca

Library and Archives Canada Cataloguing in Publication

Louttit, Ernie, 1961–, author
     More Indian Ernie : insights from the street / Ernie Louttit.
ISBN 978-1-895830-82-8 (paperback)

     1. Louttit, Ernie, 1961-. 2. Police--Saskatchewan--Saskatoon--Biography. 3. Native peoples--Saskatchewan--Saskatoon--Biography. 4. Street life--Saskatchewan--Saskatoon. 5. Marginality,

Social--Saskatchewan--Saskatoon. 6. Saskatoon (Sask.)--Social conditions. I. Title.

HV7911.L698A3 2015   363.2092   C2015-903710-7

Editing by Roberta Mitchell Coulter.
Cover design, interior design, and layout by Jamie Olson, Olson Information Design.
Cover photograph courtesy of The StarPhoenix, Saskatoon, SK
Printed and bound in Canada by Friesens.

Canadä

UBC Press gratefully acknowledges the financial support for our publishing program from the Government of Canada (through the Canada Book Fund), the Canada Council for the Arts, and the British Columbia Arts Council.

MORE INDIAN ERNIE:
INSIGHTS FROM THE STREETS

BY
ERNIE LOUTTIT

PURICH

DEDICATION

To the teachers who taught me to read and write, red ink and all.

To all the first responders and others I had the privilege and honour to work with over the years: the police officers, paramedics, and firefighters who serve selflessly and stoically everywhere in our great country, and anyone involved in the justice system in any capacity. Justice is an emotional and difficult area to work in.

To the people in our communities who care and try to make a difference, including the many First Nations that allowed me to speak to their communities in the past year and a half.

To my wife, Christine, and the many members of our two families (yes, Zak, even you).

Finally, to Don Purich, Karen Bolstad, and everyone at Purich Publishing who patiently tolerated my lack of technical savvy and slow typing to get this book out.

Acknowledgements

There are so many people I want to acknowledge for their kindness as well as their contributions to this book.

I would like to thank my wife, Christine, and my children for being patient and for distracting me when I needed distracting.

Don Purich and Karen Bolstad of Purich Publishing lit a fire under me to get this second book completed, as did people all over the province of Saskatchewan, from Dillon to Regina, who listened to me talk about the first book and wanted to know when the second book was coming—there was no pressure there!

As I have learned since leaving policing, there is a tremendous amount of work involved in publishing a book. Many people are involved in the process at nearly every stage after the first draft of the manuscript is done. Bobbi Coulter, the editor, and all of the people involved in the proofreading, layout, and design, I thank you.

To the people who read books, thus supporting writers and publishers, I cannot thank you enough. I had no idea how many people read voraciously in Canada. Reading was always an individual experience for me, so speaking at book clubs was one of the most pleasant surprises after I wrote the first book.

The private and governmental organizations that support literacy and writing also deserve thanks. I would particularly like to acknowledge the Saskatchewan Book Awards for their work promoting Saskatchewan writers. Again, this is one of those things I had no idea about when I was working the streets.

From radio to television to print, the media has been very kind and generous with me, and I thank everyone in the industry who gave me the opportunity to be heard. As well, 750 Melfort AM radio deserves a salute for the great background music while I was writing. I know a lot more about the state of agriculture now. So Saskatchewan.

I was still learning when I wrote the first book, and in all the excitement, I did not write any acknowledgements. I would like to acknowledge and thank everyone who is in any of the stories I have written for whatever contribution you made, from instilling some insight in me to scaring me into being wiser, or just showing me who you were.

Lastly, I would like to thank the people in all the emergency services who step up and fill the gaps when guys like me move on. Your service has allowed me the opportunity to tell these stories.

If I have forgotten anyone—and I'm sure I have—I apologize. You are all in my thoughts.

MORE PRAISE

"While Louttit is an active patrol officer at each crime, the best thing about this book is the stark intelligence of his opinion regarding every case. Sharing his leadership principles, Louttit's honesty will forever change our opinions about the police force."
— Linda Alberta, Prairie Books NOW #61 Spring 2014

"The 190 pages of Indian Ernie left me wishing it was 590 or even 690 pages. ... Louttit's book is not just terrific, but terrific in ways I never expected."
— Les MacPherson, The StarPhoenix

"Inspiring, fearless, unshakeable, worthy of emulation—these are all words that describe Ernie Louttit. Gritty, vibrant, engrossing, and utterly engrossing— these are the words that describe Indian Ernie."
— Saskatchewan Book Awards Jurors

1978 to 2013: not all the scars are on the outside. *Source:* The StarPhoenix

CONTENTS

DEDICATION V

ACKNOWLEDGEMENTS VI

PREFACE 1

CHAPTER 1 ■ PULLING THE PIN 6

CHAPTER 2 ■ SERENDIPITY, OR HARD WORK? 12

CHAPTER 3 ■ MENTAL HEALTH 20

CHAPTER 4 ■ CRASH 32

CHAPTER 5 ■ IMPAIRED....................................... 42

CHAPTER 6 ■ THE BALDWIN, THE BARRY, AND THE ALBANY....50

CHAPTER 7 ■ CLOSED DOORS 60

CHAPTER 8 ■ EUNDEM METAS (WE NEED EACH OTHER) 66

CHAPTER 9 ■ GOT TO BE OUT THERE................................71

CHAPTER 10 ■ CHECK YOUR EGO AT THE DOOR..................... 79

CHAPTER 11 ■ ROBBERY 87

CHAPTER 12 ■ MEASURED RESPONSE 94

CHAPTER 13 ■ NO PRETTY WOMAN SCENARIO 102

CHAPTER 14 ■ INQUIRY?....................................... 111

CHAPTER 15 ■ NOSEY NEIGHBOURS 117

CHAPTER 16 ■ NO WARRIORS HERE 122

CHAPTER 17 ■ WITH A CLICK....................................128

CHAPTER 18 ■ BE YOUR OWN SUCCESS 134

CHAPTER 19 ■ LEARNING TO LEAD 140

CHAPTER 20 ■ WHAT DO YOU NEED? LEADERSHIP 146

CHAPTER 21 ■ STREET CHECKS 157

CHAPTER 22 ■ GUNS 164

CHAPTER 23 ■ THE OTHER OFFICERS 172

CHAPTER 24 ■ HIGH..181

CHAPTER 25 ■ COCAINE AND METH 189

CHAPTER 26 ▪ COURTS, MARK YOUR ARCS 194

CHAPTER 27 ▪ VOIDS..201

CHAPTER 28 ▪ ALWAYS A CHANCE 207

CHAPTER 29 ▪ SLIGHTLY DENTED BUT GOOD TO GO 213

CHAPTER 30 ▪ POST POLICE 221

BIOGRAPHY 224

PREFACE

I TOOK AN OATH of allegiance to serve Her Majesty the Queen and her representatives on December 11, 1978, at the age of seventeen. From that point on, until October 29, 2013, at the age fifty-two, I wore a uniform, either as a soldier or a police officer. I have held a variety of ranks: private, corporal, master corporal, constable, and sergeant. I had a variety of numbers assigned to me. The last was 342, the badge number assigned to me by the Saskatoon Police Service. Behind the ranks and numbers was my name.

I am Ernie Louttit. I was born in Northern Ontario. I am a member of the Missanabie Cree First Nation, though I was only there a couple of times when I was younger. I grew up in Oba, a small hamlet almost a thousand kilometres north of Toronto. I am married to Christine, and we have four grown children: Garret, Gabrielle, Genna, and Glen. When I moved on from policing, I wrote a book about some of my experiences and my perspectives on leadership and policing. The goal was to be candid and give people who were not in policing a different point of view to ponder. I also hoped to give serving police officers a chance to think about how they are seen by one of their own former peers.

This book is my second opportunity to tell some of the stories that shaped me into the man I am and a second opportunity to give people some perspective on the men and women who protect them. I feel blessed for this. The stories here are my views and perspectives. From coal-oil lamps and woodstoves to in-car cameras and in-car computers, I have covered a fair bit of ground to get any insights I might have to offer.

I admire everyday courage and believe most people will be courageous when it matters. Effective leadership is important no matter what type of work you do or trade you are a part of. Our differences become less different as we talk about them. I think reading and teachers are as important as any army or laws are to our future.

I do not believe the world is falling apart. Instant news can make us feel it is, but it is not. Headlines from the newspapers in the early part of the nineteenth century were filled with violence, disease, and disasters, just as they are now. We live in one the best countries in the world, but there are some dark aspects. It is just part of the reality. At least no one will kill us for writing, reading, and learning. I am humbled and grateful to be part of it.

First responders deal with people, and every interaction is a multi-layered story with everyone involved having their own perspective at the end of the incident. Every victim, every offender, and every responder brings their own set of values to what they do and see. There are many police officers who have stories they should write. Their accomplishments are important and affect us all. Their humility, or thinking they were just doing their duty, stops them, or maybe they just do not want to revisit events that changed them. For me, it has been therapeutic and a salve to open some images that just will not let themselves get filed away.

My last night on the streets as a police officer was eventful. I had committed to my first book, which was due out in November of 2013. The publishers had contacted the StarPhoenix, Saskatoon's daily newspaper, and asked for permission to use some pictures that had appeared in the paper for the book. I had already agreed to take a reporter and photographer with me for my last night on patrol, and in addition to providing photographs to the publisher, on the eve of the ride-along, the paper asked to run an excerpt from my forthcoming book.

We meet at the station. Betty Anne Adam is a ground-breaking Aboriginal reporter, and Gord Waldner, the photographer, has the knack of capturing the essence of a story with one click of the camera's shutter.

What was supposed to be a trip down memory lane and a photo-op started off nice and slow. A possible drug overdose and a simple bail violation were the first two calls. We talked about past events and drove around the area I had come to know so well over the years. Gord had other commitments, and after he had taken what he thought was a sufficient number of pictures, we dropped him off at the newspaper's building.

Betty Ann and I went back out onto the street. Then the wheels fell off, so to speak. A call came in that a man had been shot. We went to the call. The victim who had been shot was conscious and full of gang bravado. The scene was quickly established as a small house a couple of blocks away. Before the night was over, five people reported being shot. I had to drop Betty off before things got totally out of hand. I was trying to do as much as I could without getting so drawn in that I could not leave. At the end of the night, detectives had established a possible address for the shooters, and together with the emergency response team, they were heading out as my shift ended.

I was by myself as the night ended, and as I went to my locker to change out of my uniform, I thought I would be more emotional, but I was not.

I unloaded my pistol. All I could think was, I made it.

I went home and fell asleep in front of the computer in the family room while reading the news.

I stopped to get gas after the newspaper article came out. The cashier told me I was on the front page. I grabbed a paper and was immediately humbled at the quality of the writing and the amount of coverage I had received. The story went viral (I've always wanted to say that!), and the attention I got was overwhelming. As a result, I decided to head to Northern Ontario to go moose hunting to get my bearings.

I woke up early one morning to head out, just as the sun would be rising, when moose start moving around. Oba, where I grew up, is a very small place, and as I was going through the town site I could see everyone's trucks in front of their houses, so I knew there would not be anyone hunting where I was. I headed up to a place called the Irving Road and was going to a ridge where I had had luck the previous year. Driving slowly, looking for moose tracks, I passed a cut road and decided to check it on my way back. I was a about half a kilometre past it when out nowhere, a Ministry of Natural Resources truck raced up behind me with its overhead lights activated.

In some remote areas of Northern Ontario, conservation officers are the only law enforcement officers you will see. During hunting season, almost everyone they stop has a high-powered rifle with them, so they are cautious. It was not a totally new experience for me to be stopped by law enforcement, but it had been many, many years. In the cities, you stay in your vehicle unless told otherwise. In the bush, I thought it was better to get out to show I was not armed. The officers' tactics were very good, one making contact and the other covering him. The contact officer asked where my rifle was. I told him it was in the truck. He asked where my ammunition was. I indicated the pocket of my jacket. He

4

then asked for my treaty card. As I began to reach for it, the cover officer, a Native man, said, "Hey, that's that cop from Saskatoon. I saw him on Facebook." We ended up talking for half an hour about law enforcement in the north. The power of the Internet, reaching all the way into this remote part of Northern Ontario, amazed me. I was now in the strange transition phase from police officer to civilian.

1

PULLING THE PIN

AT ABOUT 7 P.M. on a night shift on the first day of summer 2013, a call came in of a very intoxicated, belligerent male in the downtown transit mall, right across from Saskatoon's city hall. The other officers were tied up with other calls, and I was working by myself, as patrol supervisors always do. I had dealt with so many intoxicated people over the years, I did not think it would be problem to go to this call alone. Intoxicated persons calls are very common, and while they are not always high priority, they make the public feel insecure and reflect poorly on the police if they are not dealt with promptly, so I volunteered for the call.

As I came into the area, numerous people were going about their business or waiting for their bus. Before I could see him, I heard a man yelling. He was a tall Native man in the company of two other people. All of them appeared to have been drinking. I got out of my patrol car, scanning the crowd to make sure I had the right guy. It became pretty obvious that this male was the subject of my call. He was intoxicated enough that he did not even realize the police had arrived, in spite of his companions drunkenly trying to warn him that I was there.

I quickly formed the opinion that he was too drunk to be left on his own and that he would continue to cause a disturbance if I did not deal with him. He slurred that he was not drunk and to leave him alone. I arrested him and started to walk him to my patrol car. His friends, a man and a woman, protested, saying that they would take care of him. I warned them to back off as they tried to get between my arrest and the patrol car. The woman dragged her partner back toward the bus mall.

As I was securing my arrest in the car and advising Communications that I had a male in custody, a second, younger man staggered around the corner. The dispatcher asked for a description of my first arrest and told me that a second call had been received regarding another drunk in the bus mall. The younger man could barely stand and was using a wall for support. I went and took him into custody. There was so much going on that I did not reply to the dispatcher until I was done arresting him. All the while, the first arrest was shrieking, swearing, and protesting his arrest from the back of the cruiser. The back windows of police cars have a grated shield called window armour to prevent arrests from kicking out the windows and escaping. In the summer, the back seats of patrol cars get very hot, so you leave the windows down so the people in the back do not suffer heatstroke. Unfortunately, it allows anyone in the area to hear the streams of profanity people sometimes unleash after they are arrested.

I had now run out of handcuffs. A quick computer check revealed that the first guy had no warrants outstanding and only a couple of arrests for public intoxication. The younger guy was on bail for numerous assaults in the downtown area and had court-imposed conditions not to drink or be downtown. I now had two arrested persons to process and reports to leave, and I felt I had made enough work for myself to start the night. I wanted to clear out of the area and get these guys to the station because the arrested males were disrupting what should have been a beautiful summer evening. I turned my patrol car into the bus mall to head to the station two blocks away.

I had just completed my turn when several people pointed to two men on my right-hand side between two bus shelters. The man who was initially with the first guy I had arrested was punching another man. I stopped my car in the middle of the road and left my prisoners to stop the assault. I moved toward the aggressor. He was in a rage, and I knew there would be no reasoning with him. I told him he was under arrest and went to take his arm to secure him.

He slapped my hand away. I stepped back and sprayed him with OC spray. OC spray is oleoresin capsicum, a pepper-based irritant spray that temporarily disables a person's ability to see, and it is painful. People sometimes call it Mace. There are no long-term effects, and it is effective most of the time, though there are some people it seems to have little effect on. This suspect was one of them. I then tried to take him to the ground to gain control until a backup unit arrived. As I got a hold of an arm and a shoulder and pulled him toward the ground, he grabbed my vest, and we crashed down in a heap. Somewhere in this motion, his elbow caught my ribs on the left side and cracked two of them. I heard and felt it happen. The stakes were now raised. As I was trying to get control of the slippery, sweaty suspect, I saw a backup unit arriving at the mall. Two female constables jumped out of their car to help just as the girlfriend of the guy I was fighting kicked me square in the face. The younger of the constables took her down. Her partner threw herself into the struggle to get my guy's arms behind his back.

He dug his nails into my left bicep, and I punched him twice in the face. The strikes distracted him enough to allow me to sink a rear chokehold on him. Once he realized that the chokehold was going to put him unconscious, he surrendered and allowed himself to be handcuffed. I got off of him and stood up. Surprisingly, I was not tired, but I was hurt and I could not deny it or hide it. I picked up my radio, which had gone flying, and my notebook. My elbows and knees were bleeding from the pavement, and I must have looked a mess.

Several other patrol units had arrived, but I had not heard the radio calls because I had gotten out of the car. The man and the woman were screaming and struggling as they were escorted to waiting patrol cars. The first constables to arrive already had an arrested male in their car from a different call. Five people had been arrested in a two-block radius in twenty minutes and the platoon was only an hour into a twelve-hour night shift. But I was out. As I gathered myself, I began to look for the man the suspect had been punching. Thankfully, he had stuck around. I got his information and then went back to my patrol car, where the first two arrests were waiting.

One guy was passed out and the other was still protesting his innocence to anyone within earshot. As I was getting into my car, I could feel the eyes of all the people in the mall watching. One gentleman quietly mouthed, "Thank you." I put the car into gear and almost ran a solid red light. I braked hard, and the mouthy drunk hit his head on the screen. I apologized, and when the light turned green, I drove them into Detention.

The man and woman were still screaming and being disruptive in the sally port at the former Saskatoon Police Service building. The sally port was an area where we parked our patrol cars in the basement adjacent to the elevator leading up to the booking area in Detention. The man was yelling that he was a boxer and that I was lucky. He was muscular and had a lean build with very little body fat. The woman was screaming that all police were killers. My first arrest had settled down and accepted that he was going to sleep it off. The second guy quietly went to his cell. I removed myself from the booking area while the man and woman were booked in, hoping that they would quiet down. It was a forlorn hope: the woman yelled that she was glad she had kicked me in the face.

After they were booked in, I called the staff sergeant and told him that once I had left my reports, I was done for the night. I called home and told my wife I would be home in a couple of hours. I never came home on night shifts, especially in the summer, so my wife knew I was hurt. I downplayed it and said I had hurt my ribs again and did not tell the whole story. In pain, I left my reports and did my notes. Anyone who has broken or cracked ribs can tell you that talking, laughing, or coughing are suddenly very difficult.

My wife texted me that if I looked hurt when I got home, I was done and to put in my papers and retire. After telling the story a few times to officers coming in to check how I was doing, I finished my reports and handed in my notes and supporting documents for the charges. I felt guilty leaving, but the radio sounded relatively quiet, and realistically, I could not go back on the street.

When I got home at about eleven-thirty, I put on my best face, but some injuries are so obvious they cannot be hidden. I told the whole story and laughed even though it hurt. My kids, now all young adults, totally got it. They had been worried but joined in the laughter. I think they knew in their hearts I was almost done.

The next morning, I woke up and tried to go for a run. A run was not happening—deep breaths hurt even worse than they had the day before. I went to a doctor at a local walk-in medical clinic. I knew from experience what he was going to say: there is nothing you can do for rib injuries except take time off to heal. My knees and elbows were scraped, the middle finger of my left hand was sprained, and two ribs were cracked. The doctor said what I expected he would say, and then added that I would be out for four to six weeks. He emphasised that if I went back onto the streets before I was cleared, I would negate any Worker's Compensation claim I might file. He told me that I could not go anywhere where I could get into a fight for the entire period. I looked at him and jokingly said, "I can't even go home?" He laughed and sarcastically said, "Tough guy, eh?"

A couple of weeks before this happened, I had submitted the first draft of my manuscript for *Indian Ernie* to my publishers, Don Purich and Karen Bolstad, and we were going to meet to sign a contract two days after the incident. I made the decision that I was going to retire before I went to the meeting. I believe you only get so many luck points in your life, and I had used up a lot already. Still, it took a couple of months before I actually put my papers in. I have always said that once you say and believe the words "I am going to retire," there can be no going back. I still loved the job, and I knew it would be an adjustment. I had never been a civilian in my adult life.

All drugs come with a price. *Source:* The StarPhoenix

2

SERENDIPITY, OR HARD WORK?

AT THE START OF A NIGHT SHIFT in 2010, I booked on and, as was my habit, checked the pending calls queue on the computer. Sitting in the queue was a call requested by a detective that had been waiting for a dispatch for several hours. The call was for patrol officers to attend to an address to arrest a male for attempted murder. I had gone to the original call, to a house where an assault occurred, and the people there were not very co-operative. After we filed our report, a determined detective established that the suspect he wanted arrested had struck a person in the neck with a machete. It was more information than we had gotten the night we went to the call.

I checked to see if anyone was available to come with me. It bothered me that the call had sat in the queue for so long without someone stepping up to take it from the day shift. I was already in the area when a senior constable who was in the acting-sergeant role said he was on the way.

I was parked a block away from the suspect's address reading the report when I saw the suspect walking down the street behind me. He obviously had no idea he was wanted as he walked by. As soon as I saw the acting sergeant round the corner on the street behind me, I jumped out of my patrol car and arrested the suspect at gunpoint. Without missing a beat, the acting sergeant was out of his car and handcuffing the suspect, almost as if we had rehearsed this. In the living room of the house directly behind the suspect, there were three little faces plastered to the window. A woman, the mother I suspect, quickly hustled them away into another room. I had not seen them when I first got out of my car, but they had definitely seen us.

The wanted man had a quantity of marijuana pre-packaged for sale on him as well as cash and a cell phone. I answered it when it rang. Another male said he needed two of the good stuff. The suspect's phone was set to a site offering drug-selling tips and market information. He was very passive and resigned to his arrest. He did not say much and declined to call a lawyer. I called the detective who had the dispatch made up to let him know the suspect was in custody.

I do not know why this call sat so long without being dispatched. Anyone who checked the pending calls on the computer and chose to go for coffee or lunch instead missed a good arrest.

I went to a disturbance with several other officers at a West Side address, and during the initial investigation, I was trying to identify everyone present. One of the men there was doing his best to be invisible as the investigation progressed. He would not make eye contact with any of the officers and kept looking at the front and back doors. It became apparent that this large, muscular man was the source of the trouble. Once I turned my attention to him and he knew he could not remain invisible, he became belligerent. I asked for him for his ID. He stated that he did not have any. I watched him as he did the old eyes-right-and-left-looking-for-an-escape-route. I asked his name; he replied, "Johnny Winter." Johnny Winter was one of my favourite blues guitar players, so I knew it was game on from that point.

I asked him several more questions to try to verify his identity, but he was evasive and cocky. Satisfied that he was lying to me in the course of an investigation, I arrested him. After handcuffing him and advising him of his rights, I told him he might as well give up his true identity and deal with whatever he had outstanding. A simple "Go fuck yourself" was his reply. He would have fought if not for the other officers present at the call. I transported the sullen man to Detention, and he was booked in as an unknown person. I began checking local records on the computer. I checked incidents at the addresses we had been cross-referencing with the other people at the call for associations. I was getting frustrated because after two hours, I was no closer to identifying the guy than when I started.

Finally, I began to check traffic offences related to the other persons who were at the house. A switched-on officer had written the names of the passengers from a vehicle stop on one of the persons from the house. A quick check brought up a picture and a name for the man identifying himself as Johnny Winter. He was unlawfully at large from the correctional centre and had an outstanding warrant for escape. I went back to his cell and told him what he had been arrested for, and he looked up and said, "Like I told you before, go fuck yourself." I let the Detention staff know "Johnny Winter" would be staying for court, left my report, and went back on the street. This man had been arrested five times under the name Johnny Winter for being intoxicated while unlawfully at large. Being lazy as a street cop has never sat well with me.

Months later, I was home watching the evening news when a Crime Stoppers segment came on. I watched in disbelief as Johnny Winter flashed across the screen robbing an East Side gas station. I told my wife, "I know that guy." She just rolled her eyes. I wanted to go to the station right away, but I knew I was pushing the 24-hour policeman thing a little far. Excited, the next morning I found the detective who had the case and showed him Johnny Winter's picture from our local records. He asked if I was satisfied that this was the same person as in the video. When I told him yes, he said if I saw him he could be arrested for the robbery.

I went to the address where I had originally arrested him and, of course, was told by the occupants that he had not been seen for a while. I knew they were lying, and parked my patrol car on the same block and waited to see if I could catch a glimpse of him, which would give me grounds for a warrant to enter the house. After about half an hour, I was bored. I knew he was in the house, and I needed him to come out. Patrol officers are not case-specific, and if something happened, I would have to leave to go to whatever was going on. Suspects know this as well and often take advantage of it. I saw a man walking on the street that had an outstanding traffic warrant. I arrested the man, making sure that everyone who looked out a window could see I was now tied up with an arrest.

I took the man two blocks over and released him and went immediately back to the address. Sure enough, my suspect had left the house and was walking toward the local 7-11 store. I jumped out of my patrol car and arrested him. As I was handcuffing him, he said, "I saw you leave so I thought I had time to go get smokes." He was not bitter or belligerent this time. I transported him to jail to face the armed robbery charge.

In the late eighties, my partner and I went to the Barry Hotel and were doing a walk-through when we saw a guy by the pool table who had an outstanding warrant for an assault. As we moved in to arrest him, he decided he was going to fight us. The bar was full, and people began yelling their support for the man and his wife, who had joined in.

My partner at the time had much more experience than I and had called for another car to come into the area as soon as we walked into the bar due to how busy it was. Someone threw a beer mug at us, and people had started getting up to join in when the backup unit arrived. We got them both into custody, but not before someone broke a beer pitcher on another constable's back. The couple were duly taken to jail. It was not the last time I would see them.

In 1989, I was not yet a member of the Rider Nation, the term for the faithful fans of the Saskatchewan Roughriders, the Canadian football league's Saskatchewan team. I did not really get into football until my sons started to play in high school. Now I wear Rider socks and drive my wife crazy every game. So the day before they played in the Grey Cup that year, I had executed a search warrant after I received information that a man had reported a break-and-enter to his home and received a substantial payout from the insurance company when no break-in had occurred. The search warrant led to thousands of dollars of recovered property and fraud charges. I did not get home until after midnight. My fiancée was mad because we had plans and I was supposed to work the next morning, but I worked out a deal with the staff sergeant so I did not have to come in until 4 p.m. I could not have the whole day because so many officers had taken the day off to watch the Grey Cup. I told my fiancée I would be home on time as my overtime was getting to be an issue.

When I got to work, I overheard a radio call for a stabbing, which turned into a homicide. I was tasked to go to the scene and transport witnesses to the station for the Major Crime investigators to interview. I pulled into the lane and waited outside the tape as the patrol sergeant and another constable escorted a young man to my car. He reeked of alcohol. I was told his involvement was as a witness at this point. The young man told me in a slurred voice that he was no rat and I was wasting my time. I told him okay and drove him into the station.

In the old police station on Fourth Avenue, prisoners were driven down a ramp into the basement of the building, where they were transferred into an elevator and taken up to the Detention area on the second floor. My job was to get him up there, book him in, and turn him over to the assigned officers who were managing the witnesses. I was happy with this as I had promised to be home on time.

We got into the elevator and I pushed the button. The elevator was controlled by the Detention personnel. The elevator lurched, and halfway between floors broke down. We were stuck. It was awkward, so I started asking the man about where he was from and what he liked to do. At first he did not want to talk because I was a cop and he was not a rat. I told him we were stuck so it was going to be pretty boring until we were rescued. After a while, he began to talk about his home and his love of horses, with his boozy breath in my face. He was not a bad guy, but he had some misguided loyalties and values, in my opinion, when it came to murder and police.

Eventually, he wanted to talk about the murder. I cut him off. I did not want him talking about what happened in case he turned out to be the suspect. I did not want any defence lawyer to be able to say being stuck in the elevator was some kind of inducement for an involuntary statement or coerced confession. After a couple of hours, the elevator rose to the second floor and we were out. I booked him in and, wishing him luck, turned him over to the officers guarding the witnesses.

I was almost done, and I rushed to turn my gear in and get changed to go home. I made a quick call to tell my girl I was changing and would see her shortly. A page came across the building intercom that I was to go to the Major Crime office. With a sinking feeling, I went back upstairs. The detectives told me the guy I had brought in was refusing to speak to anyone except me because of the rapport we had established in the elevator. I was to go interview him, and get a witness statement. I was torn because it was a good opportunity to show what I could do, but at the same time I had promised to be home on time. I was not told to do anything other than get a statement, so I went up and went into the interview room. The man greeted me like a friend and provided a statement that detailed from his viewpoint what had happened.

Apparently, a group of people had gathered to watch the Grey Cup at the house of the deceased and his common-law wife. During the game, the husband kept bossing his wife around and treating her poorly in front of their friends. At one point, they were in the kitchen. She had a small paring knife in her hand, and she told him to quit being so ignorant or she would stab him. He laughed and told her to go ahead. She stabbed him once in the chest. He laughed about the poke and went back to the couch. The game ended in a Rider victory, and everyone was up on their feet cheering. The husband did not move. They checked him and saw the stab wound and called for an ambulance. In their drunken state, they figured out he was dead. My guy panicked and threw the paring knife on top of the cupboards. At the end of his story, I had him sign his statement and, quite pleased with myself, took it to the investigators.

They read it over and were instantly critical. They told me he should have been warned and given a call to counsel before the statement commenced, which I would have done if I had been told he was anything other than a witness. I left my report and went home late again and felt deflated on both issues.

The victim and his wife were the ones who had fought us in the Barry Hotel the year before. She eventually pleaded guilty to manslaughter in what truly was a situation the manslaughter section of the Criminal Code was meant to address.

After I retired, I met her at a function. I recognized her immediately, but I never said anything because sometimes meeting a policeman, even a retired one, can stir up sad memories long buried. She approached me in the hallway when I was grabbing a coffee and introduced herself. I told her I knew who she was. I had never forgotten her eyes: they reflected her intelligence and spirit. She told me she had graduated from university with a social work degree and was working on her master's degree. Her life was good, and she started to apologize for the incident in the bar so many years before. I stopped her and told her that she did not have to. We were both very different people now, and I was happy for her achievements.

In custody: the radio check-in that says all is in hand. *Source:* The StarPhoenix

3

MENTAL HEALTH

THE MENTAL HEALTH ACT, or MHA, is a provincial Act intended to help authorities deal with mentally ill people or people in mental distress. Each province has its own Act. Often when dealing with people who were emotionally disturbed or suspected of being mentally ill, my partners and I would use the police code to alert each other to the suspected status of the person we were dealing with. Police use a simplified code prefixing ten to another number designated to a type of incident. For example, ten-fifty is a motor vehicle accident. It cuts down on the air time used by the Communications section to explain each call. A simple statement like "He is 57"or "MHA" was enough to alert other police officers to the fact that the contact was out of the ordinary.

If people had any idea how many mentally ill and emotionally disturbed persons walk among us every day, they would be fearful. When I was a police officer, I dealt with those people daily, and the officers out there now still do. Most are harmless and can be truly endearing, but some are dangerous. They may harbour dark and homicidal thoughts, barely controlled by medications. They hang onto the last threads of sanity that separate impulse and action. Thankfully, they are a very small portion of the people affected by mental illness. The majority of people from my experience who suffer from mental illness do so by episodes and for the most part are able to function in society and not pose a risk to anyone but perhaps themselves.

When I first started with the police, I had not given much thought to how we deal with people suffering from mental illness. There were still institutions where the mentally ill were warehoused, and doctors there tried to help them through the bouts of mental breakdowns. The trend was just starting of medicating patients and dispersing them back into the communities.

I'm not a psychologist, nor would I ever think I was qualified to offer anything other than a layman's diagnosis of a person's mental state, but if you have ever dealt with a truly psychotic or insane person, you will never forget the experience. A human being the exact same in every way as any other, but their mind is in a place you will never know, experiencing a totally different reality than yours.

When I first started policing, and still to this day, public safety trumped everything when it came to dealing with emotionally disturbed people. Unfortunately, too many encounters with weapon-welding persons have ended tragically in the past. Some of these horrible incidents could not have been avoided, but some could have been resolved with specific training for police officers and first responders. Police forces across Canada, including the Saskatoon Police Service, have now recognized the need and have started to provide training to frontline officers to equip them to handle these volatile encounters and resolve them peacefully.

I don't know if, in the hundreds of years of uniformed policing in North America, a lot of thought went into the manner of apprehending the mentally ill who posed a risk to themselves or others. It seemed to me that at least here in Saskatchewan, no one wanted to thoroughly examine the process and how we could make it more humane and less dangerous for everyone involved. It was almost as if at the end of each apprehension, we pretended or wished that there would not be any more. I'm sure the lawmakers were consumed with making sure liability issues were resolved when granting the apprehension powers to the police. From my experience, that is where the governmental direction ended. When I went through training in 1987, we received a couple of hours' lecture on the Act and that was the extent of it. There were no specific directions or protection for the apprehenders under the provincial Act in the cases where an apprehended person was noncompliant. I could be talking out of turn, but this was my experience as a police officer.

In Saskatchewan, if a doctor or psychiatrist feels that a person's state of mental health poses a danger to themselves or others, they can swear out a Warrant to Apprehend under *The Mental Health Act*. As well, family members or caretakers can apply to a Provincial Court judge to have a warrant issued to have the subject brought before a mental health professional. Once a warrant is issued, it is the duty of the police to apprehend the subject of the warrant and transport him to a mental health facility. It sounds pretty cut and dried; however, it can be one of the most dangerous types of warrants to serve.

The process has not really changed a lot over the years: after a warrant is issued at the courts, it is picked up from the courthouse and brought to the staff sergeant, who assigns it to a constable to execute. The constable does a background check on the subject of the warrant and the address. It is important to do the background check because mental health issues are episodic and there is sometimes a possibility of previous criminal acts by the subject. After that, anything can happen.

My partner and I were given a Mental Health Warrant to Apprehend to serve on a man in his late twenties. After we made a quick plan—while reminding ourselves that the best laid plans never survive initial contact—we went to the address, a beautiful three-storey home

22

in the City Park area of Saskatoon. The family let us in and told us to be careful. They expressed surprise that there were only two of us. They directed us to the third floor, where their son's room was located. As we were going up the stairs, we could hear thumps that resonated through the entire house. We opened the door, and a young man, thickly muscled, was bench pressing two hundred or more pounds like it was nothing, steady and rhythmic, all the while saying with each press, "Because Satan says." I was content to let him tire himself out before we tried to apprehend, and at first he did not even acknowledge our presence. After twenty or so repetitions, he let the weight settle into the stand.

He looked at us with a vacant and angry look but said nothing. If he had fought, I'm sure he could've snapped us both in half and thrown us out the window. We told him he had to come with us. He looked angrier and asked why. Thinking fast, I said, "Because Satan says."

You do whatever works. He got up and walked down the stairs with us. He was taken to the hospital without any problems whatsoever.

Hoarders recently became the subject of a television reality show, but television can never capture the true nature of people suffering from this type of mental illness, or the experience of dealing with them. Their mental illness for the most part goes unnoticed by most of us for years, until some sort of crisis brings them to the attention of emergency services. By then, it is sometimes too late.

When I first started, I did not have any idea how many people suffer from this type of illness. Every couple of months, I found myself in a home piled high with clutter, be it papers, garbage, or whatever, homes where narrow paths went from room to room and the living spaces made no sense except to the occupant. There were homes where garbage had been tossed in the basement for months, where bathrooms did not work, and where cats were given free rein. Television can never capture those realities.

Most people who hoard, from my experience, are loners. Every once in a while, though, we encountered partners who somehow both suffered from whatever compulsion drives people to accumulate things and shut themselves off from the rest of us.

Unless the hoarder was independently wealthy, they generally were on disability or social assistance, and if they were not causing issues, no home visits were to my knowledge required, so this type of behaviour could go on for years until something gave. Usually it was a health issue, sometimes a fire safety concern, but always it was a crisis. In one home in which the occupant was found dead, there was barely room to get to the body. A week earlier, the furnace had been changed, without any call to health, fire, or police departments about the conditions the man was living in. I do not know if alerting anyone would have made a difference, but in this case, it could have started some sort of intervention.

One hot summer day, a call came in that a man had not been seen for several days, and a strange smell was coming from his house. I knew from experience that this was not going to have a good outcome. The day before, I had taken a similar call a couple of blocks away, which turned out to be a man who had overdosed and become almost mummified in the searing heat. When I first saw the body, I thought he was a black man. So with that image in my head, I went to this call.

When I arrived at the address, a neighbour came out and told me that the man who lived there pretty much kept to himself. It was, though, unusual not to see him at least every couple of days. The sweet, sickly smell of a decomposing body was present even in the street. I braced up and went to the front door. It was unlocked. The man, barely visible among stacks of boxes, books, and papers, was sitting dead in a worn armchair. I quickly established that no foul play had occurred and called the coroner to attend.

While searching for any next-of-kin information, I wondered as I had so many times before, how can anyone's life come to this? The man was wearing several pairs of heavy woollen socks in spite of the heat. The coroner explained that the man had died from gangrene developed from an untreated foot infection. He had no family or close friends—no one to take him to have a simple infection treated.

Things like this happen all across Canada, year in, year out. There is nothing wrong with making a call if you are worried about your neighbour, just make it in a timely manner. Emergency services will not mind, especially if the outcome is different from ones like this.

One beautiful summer day I was working a day shift when a call came in of a male in the middle of the bridge, standing on the outside of the railings and threatening to jump. Saskatoon is a city divided by bridges, and the traffic is heavy on all of them. This day was no different. I rolled up to the scene as the first officer. A man in his thirties was on the outside of the railing, holding on with one hand, and in the other he had a large can of beer. A civilian was talking to him, imploring the man come back over onto the sidewalk. Several other people were standing back, unable to pass and not wanting to leave as the incident unfolded. At first, I thought I would be sympathetic to try to get the man to come back over to safety, but he was drunk, and he knew me from previous incidents, so he started swearing at me right away.

He was an intelligent man, and I suspected this was no real suicide attempt. Based on my experience, I believed that this man was just trying to get attention, and he was succeeding. I saw the paramedics and firefighters at the boat launch area. The firefighters were getting their boat into the water. In Saskatoon, the fire department is in charge of water rescues. I let the man swear a bit more, than told him to get back over the railings so I could give him a ticket for the open liquor. He replied that he was going to jump. I told him to go ahead, but if he swam when he hit the water, I was going to arrest him for public mischief. The ticket was a bluff tactic to get a quick resolution.

He swore at me again and jumped. It was only about nine metres or so to the water. He splashed down and immediately started to swim. I jumped in my patrol car and went down to the boat launch to meet the firefighters as they brought him to the paramedics. I told the paramedics that if he was uninjured, he was mine. They could read between the lines and nodded that they understood.

He was quickly checked by the paramedics and found to be okay. I handcuffed him and arrested him for public mischief by interference with emergency services of the city of Saskatoon—emergency services were all committed to this call and were therefore unable and unavailable to respond to other calls. He protested weakly. I drove him to the Detention area of the police station to be held for court.

This whole incident was attention-seeking behaviour by the man, but I believed he was mentally ill as I had dealt with him before, and in my report, I asked for psychiatric assessment to be ordered by the courts. My experience with the system in similar situations was that if he had gone to the hospital for a psych assessment while drinking, he would have been back onto another bridge in a few hours, and ultimately the police would be called to account or be forced to intervene again. There are some situations where there is no upside for emergency services.

Months later, I ran into him again and he thanked me for charging him and said that he was back on track. For a couple of years after the bridges incident, he had some peace. His mental health problems then got progressively worse in the last years of my career, aggravated by several traumatic and violent incidents that pushed him to and over the brink. When I retired, he was still struggling with mental health issues, though he was very self-aware and candid about them.

Mental health interventions by criminal charges should be the last option considered, but sometimes, because public safety is at risk, it is the only option. The criminal charge is only the key to unlock the door to the overtaxed mental health system. Court-ordered assessments leave the subjects no choice: when their mental health is being evaluated, they cannot just walk out the door if the questions get hard. You just hoped the lawyers and the judges saw the same things in these people as you did and used the powers of court compulsion to make them get the help they needed.

Tasers, or conducted energy weapons, were not issued for general patrol duty by the Saskatoon Police Service until after I retired. They have since been used as they were intended, on violent armed persons and to stop assaultive behaviour. There have also been several incidents in Saskatoon where the weapon was deployed to prevent someone from stabbing or cutting themselves.

I responded as a backup unit to a domestic dispute one cold winter night. I knew the address well and knew the male was violent and had been to jail several times for beating the same woman. I also knew he was on a probation order not to have contact with her. There were several small children in the house as well as the woman's sisters and their children. When I arrived, two officers were talking to the man, who was standing at the front door holding a large butcher knife to his throat. The front door was open, and I could hear the women and children screaming and crying.

He saw me, and we had dealt with each other before, so I thought I had a chance at talking him down. It was a bitterly cold night and he did not have a jacket on, so I thought I might get some help from the elements as well, but after looking at me, he looked back at the constable he was talking to and cut his own throat.

He collapsed, blood gushing from the wound. The smell of blood is one of those embedded sensory experiences you never forget as a first responder. We rushed in, knocked the knife away, and waited for the paramedics, who had been staged back until the situation was resolved, to come up.

The paramedics, as always, worked quickly and got the bleeding under control enough for the man to be transported to the hospital. His blood had leaked into the snow, melting holes in it and adding a grotesque detail to a stressful call. It was difficult to get the women and children calmed down. He had given his children a picture to scar them for the rest of their lives. The man survived and after treatment was arrested for breaching his probation.

At this call, we did not have Tasers, and really not a lot of options were available. For police officers now equipped with Tasers, this is what could happen if you don't use a force option available to you because you are afraid of getting into trouble. For anyone reading a story in the news about deployment of a conducted energy weapon, as a police media reporting refers to them, on a person threatening self-harm, this kind of incident is more than likely what they were trying to prevent.

Tasers are just another tool and another option to lethal force. In the vast majority of contacts and encounters I had in the course of my career, my gun, OC spray, and baton were not even in my thought process while trying to resolve things. Circumstances will dictate your awareness of them. I am sure most police officers will tell you they experience the same phenomena.

Like all police officers, I had a healthy dose of cynicism when it came to mental illness because it was easy enough to fake in order to escape liability for criminal acts. Clever criminals and unscrupulous defence lawyers have brought forward a staggering number of syndrome defences to escape culpability for criminal acts. Every time a defence lawyer brings forward a new and unheard of type of mental illness, the Crown and the entire court system have to do an incredible amount of work to debunk the defence. Sadly, if the accused has enough funds, the farther they can go with a defence to escape liability. Recent outrageous examples include the Texas case where a sixteen-year-old from a wealthy family largely escaped culpability for four deaths he caused because of "affluenza," or Luka Magnotta claiming through his defence team that he was incapable of telling right from wrong in his murder trial. Those types of cases always get lots of media attention and diminish the commitment of people willing to support real and meaningful changes. Public education and public support is what will drive us to do better as a society when it comes to helping those people who struggle with mental health. If we think we are getting duped, support will not be as forthcoming.

Suicide and murder are the ultimate expressions of untreated mental illness. I was dispatched to a call of a suicide at an address in the west end of Saskatoon around the sixth year of my career. Dispatch indicated that a man had shot himself in the basement of his home. He had been found by a friend after not being seen for a couple of days. I met his visibly upset friend at the door, and after obtaining his information, I asked him to stay put until other officers arrived.

Death has very distinctive smell, and I could smell the deceased at the top of the stairs. There's not much you can do to steel yourself for what you're going to see, so you just get on with it. The house, as I was passing through it, had the appearance of a home where a woman had once lived and a man had been left to his own devices. The half-finished basement was neat and clean, with homemade shelves for clothing beside the washer and dryer.

The victim was seated on an old chair of the kind usually reserved for basements, surrounded by empty beer cans, with a rifle resting against his chest. The butt of the rifle was on the floor, his lifeless hands death-gripping the pistol grip and forestock. He had used his thumb to depress the trigger, and it was still in the trigger guard. The man's head was slumped forward, and there was a gaping wound in the back of it. I recognized the gun as a .22-calibre rifle similar to the guns most boys back home start off with. The force of the gun's discharge had caused blood to spray up against the wall behind the chair.

It is always an eerie and unsettling feeling to be alone with the dead, especially when the death was violent. I radioed Communications to confirm that the victim was dead. The radio seemed excessively loud when the call was acknowledged. I asked for a patrol sergeant and the Identification section to attend.

I started making notes and examining the dead man closer to rule out foul play. As I went to look at the exit wound, I realized to my horror that there was very little brain matter present. If I could have run upstairs and waited for the sergeant without losing face, I would have. Instead, I began to look for the man's brain.

I located it a few metres away, in a bucket of water with a mop. It appeared undamaged, which was remarkable given the violence of the shot to the mouth. After the sergeant and the forensic officer arrived, they explained to me that the bullet the man had used to kill himself, .22-calibre short rounds, are smaller, lower powered rounds for partridge and small game. The gas generated from firing the bullet at point-blank range had entered into and split the skull cavity. The gas had expelled the brain to where it had come to rest in the bucket. I told them that I would take their word for it.

It is still very shocking to me. The follow-up investigation revealed that the man had separated from his wife a couple of weeks previously. He left no note or explanation for his estranged wife or any of his surviving family.

There are no better safeguards in the detection and treatment of people who are emotionally disturbed or mentally ill than acknowledgment that they are in the community, and getting the community involved. As a community, the sooner we reach out or intervene, the less chance of tragedy. To simply ignore or avoid a person who is suffering only invites trouble in the long run. It can never be the job of the police and mental health teams alone. All of us have some responsibility and obligation to each other. No one should ever feel they are totally alone.

4

CRASH

UNLESS YOU ARE WALKING THE BEAT or riding a desk, a uniformed police officer's life is dominated by vehicles. You drive countless hours in some of the most extreme conditions. You drive when you are tired, after dealing with tragedies, and at speeds you would never dream of as a civilian. You have to arrive quickly to get there to help, so driving is a very important part of a police officer's job.

Police are very hard on each other when it comes to driving. One accident as a rookie will get you teased endlessly. Two or more accidents will earn you the title "Crash."

I did not drive or have a licence until I joined the army. I drove boats, snowmobiles, and motor cars on the railway, but never a car or truck. The first vehicle I drove was on an army course called "Driver Wheeled Vehicle Course"—the army liked things to sound like Army. My first ride was a jeep with a standard transmission. I stalled it so many times on the streets of Winnipeg that the instructors went directly to the bar at the end of each training day. I also learned to drive a two-and-a-half-ton truck—a "deuce and a half," as we called it—with "Armstrong steering"—no power steering. Somehow, I passed the course and was issued a military driving permit called DND Form 404. It was not a civilian licence.

If that in itself was not bad enough, the army then sent me on a course called "Driver Tracked Vehicles." I did better there. You do not really worry about accidents in an armoured vehicle.

My whole experience of learning to drive reflects the experiences of all people from isolated villages and towns. Other soldiers on the courses took driving for granted and did well. I struggled because it was all new to me, and it showed. Fortunately, most of my driving in the army was in isolated training areas or in small communities adjacent to military bases.

I have literally sunk three vehicles over the course of my career—a tracked armoured reconnaissance vehicle, a patrol car in the military police, and a patrol car with the Saskatoon Police Service—and have crashed or been crashed into by drunk drivers and stolen cars more than eighteen times. I am not going to make any excuses for my driving record. Some of my accidents were clearly caused by my inexperience or being distracted, and some I had no control over. It is part of the risk you assume as a police officer when you are out there.

The first vehicle I sank was also a leadership issue. My reconnaissance detachment had just received a totally refurbished Lynx three-man armoured carrier. I was new to the platoon, and I was the driver. Our battalion was doing a manoeuvre known as an "advance to contact." Essentially, our whole unit was moving forward, looking for the enemy force to pick a fight. We were part of the forward screen when we came to the Battle River. We pulled up and dismounted and went to the edge of the river. We confirmed the ford we were at was not defended. I could faintly hear running water but could not see any open water. I told the master corporal that the ice would not support the weight of our carrier. Our carrier was amphibious, but for whatever reason during winter exercises the plugs were removed. The master corporal agreed and radioed back our report to the company commander.

The company commander's carrier was at our position in minutes. The major came over to our NCO in a huff, and I could hear him yelling that we were delaying the entire battalion. We were to do as we were told and cross the river. Our master corporal came back and told me what I had already heard. I told him we should leave whatever we valued on the shore before we attempted to cross, including our radioman. He agreed, and with a look of resignation, he told our radioman to get out and wait until we were across the river before he joined us.

We mounted up and I started the carrier. The master corporal gave the order to advance. The clanking of the tracks announced our forward motion as we left the bank and started out onto the ice.

We were about halfway across when the carrier went through the ice. We immediately sank until the water was inches from my open hatch. I turned on both of the bilge pumps and tried to use the forward motion of the carrier to climb out. The tracks just spun on the edge of the ice, and I knew we were in trouble. I told the master corporal he could abandon ship if he wanted because it would not be long before the icy water caused the bilge pumps to fail. I could see the major on the shore, and as the red indicator light for the first bilge pump winked out, I gave him the finger. A moment later, the second bilge pump failed and the carrier sank into the river. Our guns, radios, and gear all went to the bottom.

I was treated to a winter swim in the Battle River because of a poor command decision. When I got out of the water, I was fuming and started walking toward the major. Our radioman and my NCO stopped me and probably saved my career.

Recovering our carrier was a major operation for the armoured vehicle recovery unit. After they brought it back to the hangers on the base, they got everything to work except our vehicle's heater, so we spent the rest of the exercise driving around in a freezer.

The major continued to make bad decisions and was shut down by the brigade commander when he tried to deploy our unit into conditions so extreme that they were unsafe to operate in, even for Canadian soldiers. Major Cross-Where-I-Tell-You-To disappeared after the exercise and was reassigned to run the regimental museum.

The second vehicle was a military police patrol car. I think the statute of limitations has run out on this one. The incident occurred on an air force base in Winnipeg. The Mobile Support Equipment section (MSE), or people in charge of wheeled vehicles, had flooded an area during the winter for skid-recovery training. Several feet of water in Winnipeg in the winter quickly becomes a skid pad, allowing drivers to train for driving on ice. One night shift, it was particularly quiet and absolutely frigid, so I ventured out to the skid pad with my propane-powered Ford Granada—the military was not very committed to providing the military police with real police cars in 1985. Underpowered and ridiculous looking, They, along with Chrysler K cars, were what we had to drive.

I got out onto the ice and began doing donuts, side slides, and braking turns. I justified it to myself as meaningful training, when all of a sudden I was through the ice into about one metre of water. I was hopelessly mired, and I knew I was going to be in some sort of trouble. Looking up, I saw a front-end loader doing some clean-up at the end of an adjacent runway. I went there and sheepishly asked the operator, who thankfully was a re-mustered infantryman, if he could pull me out. He started laughing but quickly drove over and chained my car out. It was bitterly cold and the car barely moved. It was making awful noises as the water began freezing in the suspension.

I limped the barely operable patrol car to a vehicle bay where we washed our cars and hoped I did not get a dispatch call. Once there, I quickly tried to hose out the ice with a high pressure hose. My shift was almost over so I was working against time when an alarm call came in. I had to go, so I limped the car to the call. When my shift was over I went back to the guardhouse. I thought I could leave the car running for the day shift and the heat would take care of things. It was a forlorn hope. The sergeant told me that the car was not going to be used that day and that I should plug it in. I did not tell anyone about my skid pad follies and went on my days off.

When I returned to work, the car was not in our lot. I assumed it was on the road, but then I saw its status on the vehicle board was out of service. I asked the night shift where the car was, and they told me not to talk about it because the military police commander was on the warpath about it. The car was apparently so completely frozen and full of ice that it had to be taken out of service. The damage was extensive and the repairs were costly. No one ever asked me if I was responsible, and I never told anyone. I do not feel absolved by this confession, but it feels good to write this and get it off my chest.

Eventually the military police acquired real police vehicles. I remember the first time I got in a patrol car with a silent partner. "Silent partner" is the generic term for the screen behind police officers that separates them from arrested suspects. The engine was powerful, and the car was full-sized. The sound of a powerful engine accelerating accelerates your heart rate as well. It just makes you feel more professional and capable.

In 1988, shortly after I was done field training with the Saskatoon Police and out on my own, I was driving past a busy downtown mall when all of sudden from the curb lane a Mercedes Benz turned right into the side of my patrol car. An older, distinguished-looking lady got out of the car and immediately flipped open an ID-holder identifying her as a senior judge with the Saskatchewan courts. She indicated she could not stay and she would deal with the accident later. I was still too new to realize I could have done the accident report later after I had all of her information. Policy at the time required a sergeant to attend all police-vehicle accidents. I refused to let the judge leave until the sergeant got there. The sergeant very diplomatically took the report and issued her a ticket for making a U-turn mid-block. Years later, I was being sworn in at a murder trial and she was the presiding judge. She made no comments or indication that we had met before. A true professional.

After the patrol car was repaired, I signed it out again. It was one of the Saskatoon Police Service's last Dodge Diplomats still in service, as they were being phased out. The car number was 45. It was underpowered compared to the new Chevrolet Caprices coming into service and was notorious for stalling in high-speed turns.

I was westbound on 20th Street and turned north onto Avenue I. I was passing by a derelict apartment building when a vehicle came shooting out of an alley at a blind corner. I had no time to react. A big North American car crashed into the newly repaired side of Patrol Car 45.

After the initial impact, I jumped out of the car and went to grab the driver. I could not see anyone. The door had not opened, and unless he had vaporized out the open window, he was still in the car. As I got up to the driver's-side door, I saw an eleven-year-old boy on the floor, high on solvents by the smell coming off of him. I literally collared him and put him in the undamaged side of my patrol car. I called for a patrol sergeant again.

The car was stolen. The boy told me that he had stomped on the gas after he had got the car started and then hopped onto the seat to steer right away because he too short to do both at the same time.

So Car 45 once again went away on a tow truck. The kid was too young to charge with anything, so he went to Social Services. About a week later, I got called in to see the inspector who was in charge of reviewing accidents to give my account. By now, the other officers had started calling me Crash. The inspector looked sternly and briefly at me as I came in. He held a file in his hands, and his eyes went back onto the file. He told me that he was reviewing the file and asked why no charges had been laid. I explained that the offender was under twelve years of age and could not be charged. He made some notes and the repeated in a loud accusatory tone, "Constable, why were no charges laid?" I could see where this was going. He wanted an outcome so he could forward it up the chain of command.

I replied that the offender was charged with the theft of the motor vehicle and ticketed for entering the roadway before safe to do so. The inspector, not looking up, made some more notes and told me I was free to leave.

I am sure if I had come back ten minutes later, the inspector would not have recognized me. If you are a leader, do not get so caught up in process that you forget to listen to what you are being told.

Central District, as it now called in Saskatoon, has had many names. Sometimes it was simply called "along 20th," referring to 20th Street, one of its main thoroughfares, or more recently "The Hood." Whatever the name, it has had a high crime rate over the years. It was also notorious as a killer of police patrol cars. Besides crashing or being crashed into, cars were vomited in, urinated in, and spat in on a regular basis. The windows were kicked out by unruly prisoners. People bled in them.

Back in the late eighties and early nineties, everyone knew the high arrest rates there were hard on cars, so as a consequence the oldest cars and the ones close to being at maximum mileage went there. As a result, I drove the beat-up cars, and given my driving record over the years, I probably did the service a favour by terminating a lot of cars earlier than anticipated. I am sure the administration and Saskatchewan Government Insurance had a different view of things.

Many accidents later, I finally got a brand new patrol car after years of driving the service's near-death cars. A brand new Ford Crown Victoria, it was by far the most powerful and superb-handling police car I had ever driven. It was like going from a propeller-driven aircraft to a jet fighter. The police model was and would become one of the premier police vehicles across Canada and North America for many years.

My partner and I were having coffee with two other officers in a coffee shop in the city's west end just before dawn at the end of a night shift. A call of an assault came in, and it sounded serious. We ran out to our car, and I jumped in the driver's seat. I was pumped at the chance to light it up and see what this car could do.

There had been reports that the computer-aided steering input was problematic in the new cars and that they would not allow correction in high-speed turns. They were vague reports, though, and they had not filtered down to patrol officers as facts. I was going lights and sirens. I approached a turn, braked hard, steered, and accelerated. The car did not correct, and we slid into thirty-centimetre curbing on the passenger side, then onto the grass. I went to put it into reverse when my partner said in his usual matter-of-fact tone, "Ernie, I don't think we are going anywhere." Both axles were broken. I broke my new car on its very first shift. The other shifts were none too happy.

Eventually, the car came back from the shop, and it was still relatively brand new. I was excited to get to drive it again. It was a night shift, and I signed out the keys. The special constable in Detention had booked off sick, and I was reassigned to work inside. The officer who was with me when I crashed the car asked if he could take it. It was not technically my car, but I gave him the keys and told him not to wreck it. A couple of hours into the shift, the troops got involved in a high-speed chase with a stolen school bus. All I could do was listen as the school bus broadsided my car, which fortunately was not occupied, totally writing it off. Sadly, I now saw the logic of giving me Central Division vehicles that were near the end of their operational life—they were almost doomed from the start.

At the start of a night shift in June 2006, a fierce storm, which have become more and more common in the prairies, struck Saskatoon. An incredible amount of rain fell in a very short period of time. The rainfall overwhelmed the city's catch basins. Streets became rivers and low-lying areas became lakes in no time at all during the deluge.

I saw a house get struck by lightning about ten blocks from where I was, and immediately there were flames. I was on the west side of a small valley occupied by a high school and townhouses. There was a small lake on the street between them. I did not think it was very deep. I was about thirty metres across it, with the lights and sirens going, when the water overwhelmed the car, stalling it. It was like a bad 1970s police chase movie—the siren slowly died and the overhead lights stopped turning.

I radioed for another patrol car to come and get me. I secured the car, waded to the opposite side, and went to the fire. The firefighters had arrived, and everyone was out of the house. A constable took over, and I made my way back to the car.

The tow-truck driver ribbed me gently as he recovered my car. I changed into a dry uniform and went back to work. The next shift, someone had put a U in front of my car number, indicating that it was a U-boat, a submarine. The car was written off. I argued against leaving an accident report but lost.

Police services, realizing the high costs of vehicle maintenance and replacement, not to mention civil liability, have taken police driver-training to a high level. Police officers are civilly and criminally responsible for how they operate police cars, so they train extensively. I was trying to figure out approximately how many hundreds of thousands of kilometres I drove without incident in police cars at high rates of speed, in pursuits or responding to emergencies, or just patrolling. Life being what it is, it doesn't matter—people remember the accidents.

Some accidents I had were just my fault, plain and simple. One winter, I saw a vehicle about five blocks in front of me. I knew the vehicle was associated with an active drug dealer. I accelerated to catch up to it so I could conduct a vehicle stop. I did exactly what you are not supposed to do on slippery winter roads on a downhill slope. I quickly lost control and crashed hard into a parked truck. The owner, who had a great and dry sense of humour, came out of the house. He told me his young son had come down to the basement where he had been watching television and nonchalantly told him, "Daddy, the police are here."

5

IMPAIRED

THE FEAR OF CRIME depends sometimes on where we live and how well informed we are. For some of us it is an ever-present concern, and for others only a remote possibility. Any anxieties we may have over being robbed or assaulted, however, pale in comparison to the everyday dangers posed by impaired or distracted drivers.

Almost all of us know someone who has been convicted of impaired driving, either as youth or when they were going through a difficult time in their lives and made a poor decision. Sadly, some of those impaired drivers will eventually kill and maim, and statistics have borne this out year after year in Canada. These people may be great people when they are not driving drunk, but when they are, they are as dangerous as any gang member.

Impaired driving is one of the most common criminal charges in Canada. It is not only alcohol that impairs someone's ability to drive. Marijuana and prescription drugs, though much harder to prosecute, are equally dangerous and impair a person's ability to drive. Impaired driving is the number one cause of criminal deaths and injuries in Canada, and it has been for many years.

It has also become a lucrative industry for some lawyers who specialize in defending accused drunk drivers. These experienced lawyers exhaustively research the laws and will challenge the evidence with a bewildering variety of defences. Inventive, clever, and sometimes outrageous, these defences have to be heard by the court and refuted by the prosecutors. The defence of impaired driving offences takes a disproportionate of the courts' time.

The initial contact with impaired drivers is almost always made by the patrol officers of a police service. They find them in a variety of ways. Some drunk drivers are reported by civilian witnesses, others are detected when they have been involved in an accident, and others when their erratic driving is spotted by officers on patrol. The Patrol division is usually populated with more junior officers, with experienced officers and sergeants sprinkled in. Impaired driving investigations are where many officers gain much of their initial investigative experience.

The legal challenges start from the moment an officer activates the emergency lights on the patrol car. The first question is, did the officer have the legal right to stop the vehicle and its driver? Every action, from the stop until the conclusion of the investigation, including the release of the driver if they are charged, is brought under intense scrutiny by the defence. The Crown Prosecutor's Office also reviews the case prior to the courts setting a trial date to see if any investigative steps were overlooked by the police. Given the costs associated both in case preparation and court time, it is the prudent thing to do.

The inexperience of some officers is seen as an exploitable weakness by many defence lawyers. Being humiliated in court by a mean-spirited counsel is an experience most officers will not be anxious to repeat, but repeat it they must if they want to get better. If your case gets tossed because an "industrial" impaired-driving lawyer found a technical violation or clear fault in an investigation made in good faith, you should not be deterred. First off, it is not your case—as an agent of the Crown, you gathered the evidence for the Crown to make its case. If the evidence you gathered for the Crown fails to meet the threshold to secure the conviction, learn from it. Get hungry for knowledge and get professional.

I heard many police officers over the years say that impaired drivers are not worth the hassle it takes to convict them. I have said it myself. An impaired driving investigation can take the arresting officer off the street for a minimum of three hours, sometimes more. The case also requires a breathalyser technician for at least an hour. On a busy night with low manpower, those officers can be sorely missed. Top it off with an intoxicated person breathing all over you in close quarters, telling you that you have ruined their life and that they pay your wages, it is not much of an incentive to hunt down drunk drivers on your own initiative.

Some impaired drivers know what buttons to push to make officers impatient and make mistakes in order to get themselves acquitted. They will prolong their search for a lawyer into hours and demand to speak to one specific lawyer who specializes in impaired driving but cannot be reached in spite of numerous attempts. People will try and say just about anything to get out of impaired driving charges, for a good many reasons. First off, most people depend on their ability to drive to maintain their employment, and to be deprived of that right is a very public punishment. People will spend enormous amounts of money defending themselves against impaired driving charges.

Even after your investigation is done, the paperwork consumes more time, and your partner ends up working alone for hours at a time. Months later, you get a court notice and will inevitably spend hours in court testifying and explaining what and why you did what you did. In one case, the defence lawyer kept me on the stand most of the court day even though he knew I had cracked ribs from a fight on my night shift and that long periods sitting were painful for me.

So how does a police officer stay motivated to pursue and investigate drunk drivers? Because the drunk driver who runs over a child on a bicycle or hits an innocent person driving home from work will not be your first impaired driving case in a year. Because you took the lumps and developed the patience needed to remove dangerous drivers from the streets. You do not escape your duty or responsibilities because the task at hand is difficult and frustrating. You have no choice and have a duty to protect us all.

On a warm summer night shortly after I started with the Saskatoon Police Service, I was paired up with a more experienced officer who had a couple of years on me. In policing, a couple of years is a lifetime when you are learning. I had just finished field training and was considered good to go as a police officer. No matter what anyone says, when you are in the first five years of policing, you still feel new.

A call came in after the bars had closed of an accident with injuries. Dispatch indicated that a car had crashed into a retaining wall just over a bridge beside one of the oldest schools in Saskatoon. Rolling up on the scene, it was very clear that the impact had been devastating. A Volkswagen sedan had been spilt in half and the backseat passengers thrown onto the roadway. There was a woman in the front passenger seat, and the driver's seat was empty.

Even at two o'clock the morning, a crowd was gathering. Firefighters and paramedics were arriving as my partner went to the injured persons on the road. The woman was still in the front seat, in shock and still seat-belted in. I took out my knife and cut the jammed seatbelt. (This is why police officers carry sharp knives.) As I was cutting her out, a man came up, obviously drunk enough not to see me, and told her, "You tell them I wasn't driving." Once she was freed, I turned her over to the paramedics. I saw the man who told her to lie to us trying to mix into the crowd. I pointed him out to my partner as a firefighter grabbed me to help perform CPR on one of the backseat passengers lying on the road. More units arrived, and my partner found the man who had spoken at the side of the car and established that he was the driver independently of me and arrested him. I told him what had happened at the vehicle. His face lit up. Proving who was driving can sometimes be the most difficult part of impaired driving accident with injuries when the driver gets out of the vehicle before the police arrive. To have him admit unwittingly to driving sealed the deal, or so I thought. The accused took the case to the Court of Queen's Bench. After a flurry of objections and legal motions, I was able to testify to his utterance, and in conjunction with all the other evidence, he was convicted. I do not recall any remorse on his part. It was something I would see over and over again.

Two days before Christmas in the early nineties, I was working a night shift when a call came in of a head-on collision on Circle Drive in the west end of Saskatoon. I hit the lights and siren and arrived within a minute or two. Like all accidents, it looked chaotic when I rolled up. I could see the two damaged vehicles, and there were people from several vehicles who had stopped to help. As soon as I got of the patrol car, witnesses began to point at a large North American car with front-end damage, saying that the driver was drunk. I looked over and saw that the driver appeared to be unconscious. I did not know if he was injured.

The second vehicle was an early model Ford Festiva, a small car by the standards of the time. The driver was definitely injured and in need of medical attention. I could hear the comforting sounds of sirens and could see the flashing lights of the firefighters and paramedics, then the red-and-blue lights of police vehicles coming to help. I spoke with the driver of the Festiva and told him help was coming. I could not smell alcohol on him at all. I kept my eye on the other driver as well.

The driver of the Festiva was a young man. He was surprisingly calm. I kept him talking so he would not go into shock. He told me he was married and was delivering pizzas as a second job so his kids could have a better Christmas. His small car had been hit head on. The lifesaving engineering of the car allowed the front end to crumple without excessive penetration of the passenger compartment. If the car had been ten years older, the engine block would have probably killed the driver.

Once the paramedics and firefighters began assessing him, I went over to the other vehicle. It was obvious by the evidence at the scene that this was the offending vehicle. It had crossed over the centre line and collided head on with the Ford. One of the witnesses, a woman, came up and with barely concealed disgust told me that the driver, a man in his forties, had gotten out of his vehicle after the collision, seemingly unhurt. He then urinated at the side of his car and, hearing the sirens and seeing the stopped witnesses, got back in his vehicle. He then pretended to pass out.

I came to the driver's side and could smell alcohol in spite of the coolant leaking out of the vehicle. The passenger compartment reeked. I could not see any obvious injuries on him, and I formed the opinion that he was feigning injury to avoid arrest. I asked him abruptly for his driver's licence and registration. He refused to answer, staring back with glassy eyes and an open mouth. I stepped back and wrote down his plate number while the paramedics checked him out.

In cases of impaired driving where the suspected drunk driver has to be taken to the hospital, an officer rides with the suspect in the ambulance to ensure the continuity of the evidence of impairment. The legal requirement for a police officer during an impaired-driving investigation is to maintain a constant visual surveillance of the suspect to ensure he does not ingest anything. No matter how obnoxious the suspects are or how despicable the deeds, they are yours until they provide a breath or blood sample or refuse.

Running the licence plate of his car revealed that he was a criminally prohibited driver for impaired-driving convictions. Once we were in the ambulance, he started listing off all his injuries to the paramedics. They shook their heads when he was not looking to let me know that they did not believe him either. Refusing to accept personal responsibility is a common trait of serial impaired drivers, and this man was no exception. He refused to talk to me and said nothing was going to happen until he talked to his lawyer. He never once asked about the other driver.

Once at the hospital, the emergency room, as always, was busy, and because he did not appear to have any life-threatening injuries, he had to wait his turn to be examined. Sometimes with impaired drivers, the waiting period before a breathalyser test is the time when you can see the person instead of the offender. You still do your job, but sometimes you get some insight into the person and how they came to be in the situation they are in. People make mistakes and exercise poor judgement, especially in impaired-driving cases. They are still people, and this may be the only contact with the legal system they will ever have in their lives, so it can be traumatic.

This man had been down this road before and knew he would probably go to jail if convicted, given his record. Even though he was on a gurney, he repeatedly demanded to call a lawyer. I told him I could not guarantee his privacy given the fact that we were in an emergency room and that I was required to keep him in my sight at all times. He insisted and had his lawyer's card in his wallet, so Security brought a phone and I called his lawyer and explained our situation. He asked to speak to his client even though I told him I would be in the room. After a couple of moments, the suspect hung up.

A doctor came and examined him. The doctor confirmed that, as I had suspected, he was not injured and released him to me. I took him to the Saskatoon Police Service, where he provided breath samples with readings over three times the legal limit even though the collision had occurred almost two hours earlier. I charged him with impaired driving causing bodily harm, driving with a blood alcohol level over .08, and driving while prohibited. He was placed in a cell and held for court. No remorse was displayed and never a question about the other driver. He told me I was the young smartass cop who would get what was coming to me. He pleaded guilty and got a three-year sentence. I suspected that the drunk driver would suffer in jail from alcohol withdrawal. He was an alcoholic who drove regardless of the consequences, with the opinion he had done nothing wrong even after the cell door closed. The man delivering pizzas so his kids could have a better Christmas recovered.

A 2014 court ruling in Alberta led to charges being dropped in an impaired driving causing bodily harm case because the suspect was not given a private call to counsel at the hospital. It was almost the exact same scenario as I experienced. I wondered if the officer had given him a private call, the defence would have used the window of time the suspect was unobserved to claim he had ingested something that affected his blood alcohol level.

I do not know how many drunk drivers I investigated and charged over my career, but it is easily over four hundred. The highest blood alcohol reading I remember was .280, over three times the legal limit. Other officers I worked with had arrests with even higher numbers. One of my former partners consistently arrested more than a hundred drunk drivers a year for years. Many of these arrests were tragedies averted.

6

THE BALDWIN, THE BARRY, AND THE ALBANY

WHEN I FIRST CAME TO SASKATOON in 1987, there were three hotels that were the ground zero of criminal activity in the Riversdale neighbourhood and downtown Saskatoon. There were other hotels where there was trouble, but those troubles were just the ebb and flow associated with any bar or drinking establishment. The Baldwin, the Barry, and the Albany were all hotbeds of drug dealing, prostitution, and the resulting related crimes. All of these hotels were built at the turn of the century and had histories as successful enterprises in the early years. Somehow, they drifted into seediness and criminality.

The Baldwin Hotel, located in the Saskatoon downtown behind the present day provincial courthouse, was the base for one man who had his share of followers. He was well liked and very intelligent as well as criminally devious. I encountered him frequently when I was walking the beat. He wore a "Billy Jack" hat and usually had some part of his daily attire adorned with a feather or some traditional link to his past. He was not a big man—you could even say skinny if you got right down to it, especially when he was using IV drugs—but for whatever reason, he commanded respect in his circle, and his followers were fiercely loyal to him. He appeared to be in charge, at least at the Baldwin. One of his many women told me years later that every time I walked into the bar, he would hand her his gun to hide. I knew he was a criminal, and in spite of that, I felt he was a wasted leader, capable of so much more than what I was seeing. The extent of his influence became apparent to me when a loud drunk or a young guy trying to make an impression would try to start a fight with me and, with a simple gesture, he would shut them down.

He stabbed a woman in the leg for reasons the victim never clearly articulated, and a warrant was issued for his arrest. I arrested him on a day shift right in front of the old courthouse on 20th Street. He had a small bird in his jacket when he was arrested. He told me not to judge him because it was not my place.

He was murdered at the Albany Hotel, stabbed to death in a barroom full of people by a brother and sister, shortly after he got out of jail. I'm not sure if the Albany was any one group's hotel—it seemed to be almost the free-trade hotel for criminal groups.

I was off duty when the murder happened, and when I returned to duty, I was called down to the Major Crime office. The detective in charge told me that a band was videotaping their performance when the murder took place and asked if I would watch it to see if I could identify people on the tape as potential witnesses. At the time of the murder, the band was trying to play the song "Roxy Roller" by Sweeney Todd. It was awful. I watched and listened to the video for hours, picking out several people by name. To this day, if the song "Roxy Roller" comes on the radio, I immediately shut it off.

Informants were the only way to get insight into the drug and prostitution rivalries going on at the time. People were giving me information and intelligence that was helping me get a picture of what was going on, but unfortunately, events were moving faster than my ability to use the information.

I had been in contact with the woman accused of the killing and her group many times up to this point. She almost seemed untouchable. I would lay charges, and her underlings would take the rap or witnesses would not show up for court. I even did a search of her house, where the other officers and I seized a loaded, sawed-off 12-gauge shotgun and a loaded, sawed-off .22-calibre rifle from under the mattress of the bed she shared with her common-law husband. While we were doing the search, she shrieked, swore, and muttered at us. Her young son—I don't think he was even twelve years old yet—told her, "Shut your mouth, cunt, and let the pigs finish and get out." In the presence of evil or not, it still shocked me. Somehow, her common-law husband took the charge for the gun charge and was sentenced to forty-five days in jail. She walked free again. Her common-law husband was eventually murdered, beaten to death with a baseball bat. She could not get out of the murder charge from the bar, or so I thought. She and her brother pleaded guilty to manslaughter and after serving their time disappeared from Saskatoon for a few years.

The Barry was controlled, as far as I could tell, by one family and their people. Absolutely ruthless to their prostitutes and enemies, they went to great lengths to ensure informants did not flourish. I arrested some of the crew from the Barry, but never for the core offences I suspected they were responsible for. The team approach to investigating them just never seemed to materialize, so they just faded from sight. They will have a reckoning someday, and the police will have nothing to do with it.

In spite of all the things happening in the bars of these hotels, there were many people who lived in the rooms above them. The renters were a very mixed crowd: Old criminals who had no place else to live. Young criminals who could not find any place that would take them. Men who, for whatever reason, had no family. Many of them told stories about the good old days when criminals had respect for each other and the code of the streets. They would talk about the active criminals and how reckless they were. I am sure that many exaggerated their criminal prowess. One man even told me that he was in Attica penitentiary in the United States during the riot that killed more than forty prisoners and guards. I never called him on it because it was important to his sense of self-esteem and it did not really matter either way.

Most of their meals were made on hot plates in their rooms, or taken in soup kitchens or at the Friendship Inn, the community kitchen serving meals to those who needed them. They took it in stride when police were in the hallways, and I am sure we offered some entertainment value as well. If one of the long-term occupants was mean-spirited or committed crimes against the others, we almost always got the nod from someone if they were back in their rooms when we came looking. The hotels were their homes, and you needed to look after where you lived and in turn be a good neighbour.

There was one fellow staying at one of the hotels who stood out for me over the years. How we met was a story in and of itself. I was on patrol early in my career and was close to the end of a day shift when a woman ran out of her house and yelled at me that someone had just broken in through her back door and he had a knife. We were still using old Motorola portable radios back then that weighed about over two kilograms. The batteries only lasted about ten hours into a twelve-hour shift. I got out of the car and told woman to get behind me. I went to call it in and realized my portable radio battery was dead. I did not want to get back in my car to call Dispatch in case I lost the bad guy. I pulled out my pistol and my pepper spray and went in the house. I cleared the living room and went toward the area of the back door.

All of a sudden, a closet door flung open and a male with a

knife raised over his head was coming toward me. I sprayed him with OC spray. He flew backwards and crashed heavily to the floor. For a second I thought I had shot him with my gun as well as the pepper spray. It would've been a sympathetic reflex. I holstered my gun and went to check on him. He was making a lot of noise, obviously in great pain. I quickly looked over his face and realized that I had not shot him. I handcuffed him and then saw a second male coming through the back door with a baseball bat. I ordered him to stop but he didn't, and I sprayed him with OC spray as well. He ran a little bit but he could not see, so I quickly caught and handcuffed him. It turned out that the guy with the knife had broken into the woman's house because the guy with the bat was chasing him over a drug debt. The reason the guy with the knife reacted so strongly to the OC spray was because he only had one eye and the stream of spray went directly into it.

When I was booking him in after decontaminating his good eye, he told me he had been stabbed before, but the spray was the worst. He had never felt pain as intense before. He was an old rounder, a term used to describe career criminals. He stuck to the old codes and told me he only did dirt to other criminals. He apologized for breaking into the woman's house—he didn't like his lifestyle to affect civilians. He passed away at one of the hotels alone in his room years later. He was almost symbolic of the type of resident the hotels housed. Over the years, he gave me lots of direction and advice without ever betraying his code by giving specific names. We became friends, as much as a cop and semiretired career criminal can be.

Bar checks, where the police do a walk through the bars looking for wanted criminals, were so common at these establishments that everyone except the wanted criminals took them for granted. You were supposed to call for another patrol car so you would not be alone when you went in. Circumstances did not always allow that to happen, and sometimes other officers were tied up at other calls, so a lot of times I went in alone—not a practice I would recommend to young officers as things can go south pretty fast. Luckily, there are not many bars or hotels like these places in Saskatoon anymore, but for a police officer, bars and nightclubs can be very dangerous places. Weapons can be concealed more easily. There are always more people than police. Inhibitions are lower, as is the lighting, and drunk people are always braver and more likely to insult or bait police when they are with their friends.

Just before one o'clock on a day shift, I went to check on the patrons in a bar behind the courthouse, the Continental. As I entered the bar and let my eyes adjust to the smoky dimness, I saw a male I had arrested on the previous night shift for an assault. He had other charges pending for robbery and escape. I knew he had conditions on his bail that prohibited him from entering a licensed premise or consuming alcohol. He was a big guy. I asked him to go with me to the front of the bar so I could check his conditions.

At first, he was compliant, but something wasn't right. He was displaying all the classic signs of flight, shuffling his feet and looking for an escape route. After confirming his conditions, I touched his arm and told him he was under arrest. He shoved me and tried to run out the door. I got a hand on the back of his neck and began to push him down to the sidewalk. He was way bigger and stronger than I am, and he managed to spin around, grabbing me by the bottom of my legs and throwing me into a truck parked in front of the bar. He had me pinned there, but my arms were free. I managed to get my OC spray out and gave him a quick shot. He let go of my legs and started running. After he dropped me, I called for backup and started chasing him. As he ran,

I struck his legs with the baton, and he turned toward me each time. I had dropped my pepper spray when he let go of me at the truck, so we were standing face-to-face, I think both trying to decide what was next. He was big enough for me to know that I would have to hurt him if he came at me again. Suddenly two bike patrol officers came screaming up and did a flying tackle on my suspect from their bikes, and we took him into custody.

There had been a string of armed robberies in Regina by a male who blackened his face with shoe polish, but the Regina police had identified him. My partner and I were doing a walk-through of the Albany Hotel, and as we came out, I saw the suspect with another man. I quickly grabbed the man the media called the "black-faced bandit" and arrested him. His companion took off to the Barry Hotel across the street. He matched the description of a male responsible for an armed robbery earlier in the day in Saskatoon. We asked for another car to come and get our arrest so we could identify the other guy before he got away.

After we turned over the Regina guy, we went into the Barry. It was busy, as it always was on paydays. I saw the suspect at a table with several other people in the middle of the bar. He was not a big guy. He had fiery red hair and was defiant and confrontational from the moment we started talking to him. A quick check of his identification revealed that he had a minor outstanding warrant. The moment I told him he was under arrest, all hell broke loose. He started to fight, and the Tasmanian devil analogy comes to mind. Fast and strong, he was doing pretty well against two of us. Someone went to jump on my back, and I hit him in the mouth with my elbow. I saw a spray of blood, and he disappeared. I finally got a chokehold on the suspect and started dragging him to the floor. In the meantime, my partner had hit his emergency button because the situation was almost out of control, especially with a full barroom.

Backup officers came running in, and we eventually wrestled this wild man into handcuffs. As we took him out of the bar, I was greeted by about eight patrol cars with their lights flashing and brakes smoking. I had never been in a situation where an emergency button had been pressed. The response was humbling. These officers had come full bore.

The first arrest was eventually sent back to Regina, where he pleaded guilty and was sent to the penitentiary. The wild man was never identified for the Saskatoon armed robbery and received a short jail sentence for assaulting police and resisting arrest. He moved out of Saskatoon shortly afterwards.

The Barry was the scene of one my best lessons about the court process. I was called into the Major Crime office and asked to go to the Royal University Hospital to see if I could identify an injured male who was in critical condition from a head injury. He had apparently been punched by a bouncer at the Barry while being ejected and had hit his head when he had fallen on the pavement. When I got there, I immediately recognized him as a man we used to call Hook. He was a regular in the downtown bars and had a mean streak when he was drinking. He had a prosthesis on his arm with an old-fashioned hook on the end, and people who crossed him found he was always ready to use it. I left an investigation report with his real name and didn't think a lot more about it.

He eventually died as a result of his injury, and the bouncer was charged with manslaughter. Months later, I was served a subpoena from the defence. I had never been called as a defence witness before, so I called the Crown Prosecutor's Office for an explanation. I was told no witness is ever the property of either side in the judicial process. I was expected to appear and testify accordingly. I appeared in Court of Queen's Bench and testified about Hook and his habit of trying to inflict injury on people when drinking. The bouncer was acquitted. The detectives who investigated the case did not say anything to me so I never knew how they felt about it.

Shortly after we were issued OC spray, I was doing a walk-through of the Albany Hotel beverage room when I saw a male who had an outstanding assault warrant. The bar was busy, and I knew from dealing with him on previous arrests that this man would actively resist arrest, but I knew most of the people in the bar by name, so I decided to make the arrest. I told him he was under arrest, and he replied, "Fuck you I am!" and put up his fists. I had the OC canister in my left hand, and I sprayed a quick burst into his eyes. He crumpled, and I quickly handcuffed him and took him out of the bar. After he was in cells, I came back to the Albany, and the regulars began complimenting me on the speed at which I had dropped the man I had sprayed. They thought I had hit him. I did not tell them any different—in the bars a reputation for speed in a fight is not a bad thing.

At the Barry Hotel a couple of years later, I saw another wanted man who was very active in the drug trade. Our eyes met, and he ran out of the bar through the lobby door. I ran after him. I thought he had run out into the street, but one of the regulars who lived upstairs motioned that he had run into the basement. I had never been in the basement of the Barry before, and it did not disappoint. I had no idea it was so large. There was dust and cobwebs everywhere and dozens of small rooms for storage. It was very poorly lit, and there were a million places to hide. Luckily for me, the suspect had poor lungs from all his years of drug abuse, and the oppressive atmosphere of the basement caused him to start hacking. He was coughing and sweating so hard that he was not able to dump the pills he was carrying. He was arrested and charged with the new drug offences as well as the warrant.

So it went, year after year, until the Baldwin Hotel closed. The Albany was sold and converted to a halfway house for federal offenders. Still the Barry held out until 2008 when it was bought by a local businessman and demolished. Twenty-one years of arrests and bar checks came to an end.

I never understood what I thought was the official indifference to these bars. When you have problems as obvious as these places were, that is where your efforts should begin. Still, the downtown and Riversdale are better places now that they are gone.

A quick brief to the media goes a long way. *Source:* The StarPhoenix

7

CLOSED DOORS

PRIOR TO RETIRING from policing, I saw a trend toward what I consider the over-specialization of skills and the physical separation of officers through building and workplace design. I do not know if it was on purpose or just a result of a growing organization. In an occupation where the raw material of your trade is people, and communication is the key to success, it struck me as a troubling trend.

The need for control over outcome was leading to less and less officer discretion. It was as if every situation was supposed to have a pre-determined outcome or a successful resolution. In the world of policing, that is well-nigh impossible. Every situation is different and consequently so is the outcome. This can happen even if it is not the intention of the leadership because it is so gradual. I was seeing it the last years of my career in officers' reports. They would preface their decisions in reports with the fact that they had checked with their supervisors or prosecutors in order to validate their actions. Their decisions and actions were right and sound in the first place. It was troubling. The quality of police recruits is excellent. In the chaotic world of policing, insisting on outcome in a neat package every time seems unrealistic and unattainable. The personal interaction between the police officers and the people they deal with changes with every situation. Mistakes made in good faith are better than mistakes made in a rigid process.

There are many officers who are creative and find ways to resolve situations even at the risk of being admonished for their actions. Eventually though, if you are called in enough times, you will eventually rigidly stick to policy for self-preservation. There are times when you have to follow procedures and policy to the letter, but more often than not, the policy doesn't reflect the real-life, real-time situation the officers are facing. You cannot take the human element out of policing by written policy. You have to trust the judgement and ability of the officers on the street to do the right thing and hold the ones who don't to account.

When I first started with the Saskatoon Police Service, all of the constables had to do a stint in Communications as a call-taker and dispatcher. The Communications section was one large room with the dispatchers at the front and two rows of phones behind them. The Communications sergeant sat at a desk in the back and monitored the centre. There were no computer screens, and when a call came in, you wrote it on a card. Different coloured cards were used for different priority calls: green for low priority, up to red for high priority. There was a track system, and you slid the card to the dispatcher. The dispatcher would pile the cards on the desk by priority. If a hot call came in, like an accident with injuries, if you were the call-taker, you could just yell to the dispatcher to get a car going before you wrote out your card. It was very quick, and everyone knew what was going on pretty much all the time unless they stepped out of the room.

The dispatcher would go on the air and ask if there was a unit close to the incident available to go. Believe it or not, people even smoked at their desks back then—we have come a long way in that regard.

I did six months in Communications. I did not answer phones for very long before I started dispatching—if I had to be inside, dispatching was better suited to my personality. As frustrating as it was to be off the streets in the first few years of my career, being in Communications could be fun and challenging. What it did for me was give me a broader perspective of the whole organization and a career-long respect for the people who worked the Communications section.

A couple of years later, the department implemented a CAD (Computer Aided Dispatch) system. The first mobile data terminals (MDTs) were placed in patrol cars. They were little computers, difficult to read, with tiny screens and a propensity to freeze up in the winter. Prior to the MDTs, when you were dispatched to a call you had to write the call information in your notebook. In practice, you also were to write down the call information from the MDT.

The Communications section was redesigned as well. The dispatchers were physically separated from the call-takers and placed in another room. The call-takers were required to type the information and forward it on the computer to the dispatchers. Even up to the end of my career, I would watch call-takers get up from their computers to go tell the dispatcher the details of a serious call. Technology and the search for efficiency can sometimes take away from the personal interactions that make a section effective.

I had a routine throughout most of my career after about the three-year mark, which I kept up right until I was done. Whenever I made an arrest, I would transport them into Detention. Once in Detention, I would explain the arrest and circumstances to the Detention staff. Detention was next door to Communications, so I would go to Communications and tell them what had transpired. Central Records was the next floor down, so after Communications I would go there and tell either the supervisor or typists what they could expect as far as reports. If the person I arrested was a person of interest to an investigative section, I went there and told them the arrest was in Detention. Then I left my report. I did this or some variation of it every day.

It served several purposes at the same time. It helped me articulate an incident, which made for easier report writing. As well, I was teaching the special constables in Detention. I was letting Communications staff know what had happened at a call and mentally preparing the Central Records staff for what was coming. I thought it was team-building and being inclusive, but in the latter part of my career, there were more restrictions to access into Central Records and more closed office doors.

The use of e-mail to communicate would lead to hours of time in front of computers sifting through a lot of useless information when the message could have been communicated in two minutes of face-to-face conversation. I did not even know we had an e-mail system until months after it was implemented. An inspector asked me why I had not answered his e-mail, and I answered honestly that I did not even know I had an e-mail account. I was ordered to see the tech guys and activate my account. When I did, I found several thousand unread messages. I did a mass delete, figuring if any of them were important someone like the inspector would have told me. Once I did this and had a clean slate, I was caught in the e-mail vortex right until I left policing. Some messages were meant as leadership, but in a perverse way, all they did was allow someone to be critical without facing you. If you are a leader, you do not "lead" on specific personal or job performance issues using e-mail. You call the person in and address the problem—that is what leaders do.

The rise of special teams' influence over the decision-makers in police services is, in my opinion, made at the expense of the patrol officers' and patrol sergeants' ability to make timely decisions. Many tactical situations are solvable by the officers on the street. Insisting on or activating emergency response teams every time a situation is even remotely hazardous causes officers, as human nature dictates, to pass responsibility to someone else. If they are in fear of criticism from emergency response team leaders or executive officers every time they are confronted by someone with a weapon, it can create self-doubt and cause officers to second-guess themselves. Firearms have posed a risk to police officers since firearms were invented; knives, axes, and every other type of improvised weapon have been there, too. Anyone can "what if?" a situation into a crisis. I understood the need for a well-trained and equipped emergency team for reducing the possibility of injury to the suspect or anyone else in a crisis situation. By the same token, however, just because a call is violent, it does not always warrant calling a full team to deal with it.

So it comes down to balance. Sometimes it is very clear that a team is required. High-risk search warrants, and with barricaded suspects who are armed and all other tactical options are exhausted are some of those situations. I smarted over being called reckless more than a few times over my career. A lot of decisions I made in regard to armed suspects were made based on my experience and prior knowledge of the suspects. Some were unavoidable, like foot chasing a shooting suspect into a house. Confronting a knife-wielding suspect who is actively stabbing someone is a situation where highly trained and confident officers will do their duty as long as we have not taken the initiative and decision-making ability from them. Special teams are just that: special. Not everyone can be on them, nor are they always available when you need them.

I used to write up search warrants almost every week during the first few years of my career. I don't think they would be granted now the way they were written back then. I used simple, straightforward warrants, often not more than three pages long, to find stolen property, guns, drugs, and other offence-related evidence. Most officers will not write a search warrant now until they have been in the service for years. Court decisions have caused the art of warrant writing to be confined to a small group of specialized officers with extensive experience. Challenges to warrants under the Charter of Rights and new disclosure rulings require the police to produce warrants that can withstand challenges. The warrants have to protect confidential informants and attempts to reveal investigative techniques. The police now require a warrant for just about every procedure they do. An example is the requirement to have a warrant to process a crime scene even if they had lawfully entered and secured it without a warrant. All this warrant writing takes time and slows everything down. The problem is that the officers writing the warrants are so busy that the officers in Patrol are not gaining from their experience. Those officers need the experience of writing successful warrants and even unsuccessful warrants to help them become better police officers before they succumb to the temptation of letting someone else do them as a matter of course.

If you are a police officer, the learning and teaching never stops. Personal interaction with other officers, regardless of rank or speciality, fosters learning, and that learning comes out on the street with you. It can only benefit you when you are working.

Get out of the car and let people know who you are. It goes a long way and can actually protect you from assaults. People are a lot less likely to attack you as a police officer if they know who you are. It is not entirely foolproof, but outside of domestic situations, human nature makes it more difficult to assault someone if you know each other's name.

The public expects the police to be brave and decisive. If police officers are taught to be too cautious, personal bravery can be corroded, and their skills will decline with over-specialization. There has to be a balance, and finding it will be a continuing challenge. Fewer closed office doors and more interaction with each other and the public makes for a healthier organization.

8

Eundem Metas (We Need Each Other)

ST PAUL'S HOSPITAL is in the centre of the area where I worked almost my entire career. Every city has a hospital like St Paul's, a hospital where victims of violence and poverty-related misfortunes, or anyone with any kind of aliment or affliction, goes because they can get there on foot. You would think being able to walk to the hospital in our society would not be that important, but if you are poor, it is.

St Paul's, for people not familiar with Saskatoon, sits at the top of a hill in the "Alphabet City," so called because the streets are numbered and the avenues are lettered. The hospital was founded by the Order of Grey Nuns more than a hundred years ago. The staff there are second to none.

St Paul's Hospital should have been renamed the St Paul's Community Hospital years ago because it is an island, a place of safety and comfort to everyone in the neighbourhood. You could be fighting for your life outside on the streets, been stabbed or shot, but when you entered those doors, it was over. They knew all the regulars and never turned anyone away. Such was the respect the hospital and the staff had garnered over the years that I used to tell my partners at work that if I were shot or stabbed anywhere but the head (because Royal University Hospital was better equipped for head traumas), take me to St Paul's. The other hospitals in Saskatoon were equally as busy, but it was the walk-in cases and its location that made St Paul's so accessible. It was rare that I did not find myself in the hospital at least once in the four-day work cycle of a patrol officer.

The police and medical staff understood each other and the people who came to be there as patients. The unspoken communication and understanding between officers and staff was inspiring. I knew the degree of abuse the emergency room personnel took from injured people that were drunk or high. I had a rule almost everyone in my area knew once I had dealt with them, and those who did not know the rule found out quickly: if you abused the sanctity of the hospital or the staff, you were going to jail.

Every once in a while, a catheter was required, and the more experienced emergency room staff knew that that would silence the most abusive patients pretty quickly. But for the times when the abuse outweighed the medical needs of a patient at the hospital, I was always willing to take calls at St Paul's. The people who worked with and eventually for me knew the way I felt, and hospital calls almost always got prompt responses. The relationship went both ways, and when an officer was injured or in medical distress, the care was phenomenal.

Early in my career, I was the odd man out and was paired up with a patrol sergeant. He was a character. He could have been and should have been a Texas Ranger. He was not a very large man—in fact he was small in stature for the police officers of his era. He had a handlebar moustache and the look of a veteran taking it all in stride, as if being a police officer was as natural as breathing. I was not big on pairing up with sergeants, but I looked forward to working with him.

A few months earlier, I had responded to a call of a belligerent drunk at a local hotel. I had just gotten off probation as a police recruit. At the call, the drunk turned out to be a British soldier in town for the night from a local base. I was back in familiar territory from my days in the military police when dealing with drunken soldiers, both Canadian and British, was a mainstay at the base in Wainwright, Alberta. He would not settle down and was causing a disturbance in the lobby of the hotel, so I arrested him. After a bit of active resistance, his antics had attracted a large group of onlookers. In those types of situations, no matter how much the arrested person deserved to be arrested, as soon as you go hands-on to make the arrest, he will find sympathizers.

I dragged him out of the lobby to my patrol car. I had not been able to search him yet and he was still struggling, so I slammed him onto the back trunk of my car. Of course, as luck would have it, his nose hit the surface and he began to bleed profusely. I looked up and saw my patrol sergeant, who had come to the scene to check on me because I had not been on the radio since I had arrived at call. This was in the days before extended microphones, and you had to physically have the radio in your hand to transmit. In the commotion, I needed both hands.

The arrested soldier was swearing and telling the sergeant to look what I had done to him. There was blood freely flowing and all over the trunk. The sergeant calmly asked if I was all right. I said I was and started to explain the circumstances. He cut me off, said, "I like your style, kid," and nonchalantly turned, got back in his patrol car, and left. To me, he was the perfect patrol sergeant for those early years. He was knowledgeable, experienced, and as I learned, he only intervened when he had to. You knew he listened to the radio and would be there when you needed him.

The night we were working together was busy. We backed up other units at calls and generally covered a lot of the West Side. The sergeant complained about a pain in his left arm and explained that he had been doing renovations before he had come to work. I was so caught up in the tempo of the night I did not notice that he was sweating constantly and took at face value the explanation for the soreness of his arm. Finally, as we were en route to a call with lights and sirens, I could see the anxiety on his face. At first I thought it was my driving, but then he said, "I think I am having a heart attack, young fella."

I had volunteered to be a CPR instructor shortly after I finished recruit training and had started instructing almost right away. The realization that every symptom he displayed was a warning sign of an impending heart attack hit me like a kick in the face. I radioed in and raced to St Paul's, where the staff immediately started their heart attack protocol and saved his life. The smoothness and professionalism of the staff helped assure me that one of my early police heroes was not going to die. There was a lesson there for me as well: even though I was a CPR instructor, I had been blinded by my closeness to the victim. It was a lesson I would not forget.

As the years went by, I got to know many of the nurses and doctors and was always impressed with the level of care and lack of cynicism. Assault victims, accident victims, and intoxicated people who have to be checked prior to incarceration are just some of the reasons there is almost always a police presence in the emergency room. Often, someone who had been a victim of a domestic assault would decide to report the assault only after seeing an officer in the emergency room.

Sadly, in my last years on the street, the health districts put an end to the easy access and communication with the front-line health care workers by instituting strict privacy guidelines for staff. The doors to the trauma and treatment rooms in emergency were locked and you had to be buzzed in. Fearing discipline, nurses and doctors were less forthcoming with information about domestic assault victims or crime victims where there was not a mandatory reporting requirement. Unless the victim specifically asked for the police, they were required to treat and release the patient without involving the police. The mere threat of litigation rather than actual litigation shut down a valuable method of detecting unreported violent crime, especially domestic abuse.

Many doctors and nurses must have been frustrated and angered by this. Doctors and nurses, by virtue of their occupations, know more about interpersonal violence than most people. Not being able to help must be one of the most frustrating aspects of their jobs. Knowing domestic violence almost invariably escalates, hearing "I ran into a door," or "I fell down the stairs," night after night, and knowing the abuser would come to collect the victim has to be a tough pill to swallow.

I am sure there is a bigger picture here, but as a point-of-contact street cop, it was frustrating. I know the counterargument, where women who are abused will not seek medical attention after they are assaulted if they know the police will be notified, and it is a powerful argument. I have talked to women in emergency rooms who said emphatically they did not want to talk because "he will kill me." Sadly, there lies the power of the abuser, and if not stopped, the prophetic words of the victim.

As a police officer and now as a civilian, I was always troubled by barriers to victims. Sometimes the barriers were systematic and policy driven, anticipating problems instead of dealing with them. The police and medical community ultimately have the same goals of personal safety and community health. Because they have different methods of achieving them does not mean they are opposing.

9

GOT TO BE OUT THERE

SOME SERIOUS CRIMES GET SOLVED by accident. By the same token, if you were not out there on the street, these accidents would not happen.

My longest working partnership went from 1993 until 1999. By 1998 we were so attuned to each other's cues and abilities, we were like brothers. We were, in a lot of ways, opposites. He was a former teacher. He was well educated and articulate. My partner acted tactically but thought strategically. Having a partner who could keep you from getting caught up in the trap of getting tunnel vision while trying to police your assigned area was important. More than once, he reminded me that our area was not the only one needing the police, and that not everyone had the same job.

We were on our last night shift of a busy summer block and looking forward to our days off. We were taking calls and making arrests—nothing too serious, just warrants and breaches of court orders and such. The east side of Saskatoon, on the other hand, had a carjacking and an armed robbery just before midnight. We were monitoring the radio, but nothing we could act upon came across the air.

We were patrolling by a school in the Pleasant Hill neighbourhood of Saskatoon when we saw a man who was obviously drunk trying to get in the window of an apartment building. We quickly intervened. He drunkenly told us that he lived in the apartment. When we asked why he did not just use the front door, he told us that there was a guy sitting on the front steps who made him nervous.

We went to the front door to check. A guy was sitting there with a plastic 7-11 bag with a carton of cigarettes and some other items in it. In and of itself, this was not too suspicious, but having worked the area for so many years, I knew. A carton of cigarettes at two in the morning was enough to get you robbed. This is where the experience of working together for years kicks in: we both knew instinctively where this was going and what we were going to do.

I observed that he had leaves on his jacket, as if he had been lying down. My partner saw a taxi down the block watching us. The armed robbery on the East Side had occurred at a 7-11 store. The victim's cell phone had been stolen during the carjacking. A quick call to Communications staff indicated the man in front of us had been picked up on the east side of Saskatoon from the area the K-9 officer had lost the suspect from the 7-11 robbery. I called the officer who was investigating the carjacking and asked him to call the stolen cell phone. The man in front of us blanched when the phone in the bag rang. My partner arrested him. I handcuffed him and placed him in the patrol car.

We let the drunk guy in so he could go to bed, and I seized the cigarettes and cell phone. My partner was not done yet. We transported our arrest to Detention and hooked him up with a lawyer. After he was done, my partner told the arrested man that it was bad for him but it was the not the end of the world. He asked the man if he wanted to write an apology to the people he had victimized on this night. Surprisingly, he said yes and very candidly told us about the evening's events while writing a letter of apology. In the end, I felt a little sorry for the guy. He was in a tight spot and had impulsively committed two serious crimes. No mastermind, he pleaded guilty on his first court appearance.

You have to be out there for things like this to happen. I loved Patrol.

It was almost five in the morning. I was with the same partner, finishing a different night shift. We saw a man staggering down the street. We rolled up, and it was quite obvious that he was very drunk. At first, he was co-operative and seemed like a pleasant drunk. He produced his identification while weaving back and forth. He had the look and feel of a person who had seen the inside of a prison a time or two. My partner kept him talking while I checked him for outstanding warrants or court conditions. Both of us looked at each other when his name came back clear of any warrants and having no criminal record. My partner picked up on the fact that all of this man's identification, including his social insurance card, were brand new. When questioned about the identification, his mood shifted and he told us we had no fucking right to check him.

My partner patiently explained that we were concerned for his safety as his state of intoxication was such that we felt he was incapable of taking care of himself. Both my partner and I were exhausted. We only had one more hour to go and we needed to leave a few reports before we could go home on our days off. But something was not right with this guy, and my winger, in spite of being bone tired, was not letting it go. Whenever he said "Okay, pal!" to a suspect, I knew my partner was going to arrest him. I moved closer as he grabbed the suspect and told him he was under arrest. We handcuffed him, and now his demeanour was totally defiant.

We transported him to Detention and booked him in for

public intoxication. We went to work on the police computers to try to figure out his true identity. After two hours of fruitless searching on databases and questioning the man, I was satisfied that we could charge the man with obstructing police by providing false identification. Once he was charged and fingerprinted, we would know who he was and why he had lied to us. We laid the charge.

I just wanted to go home. We would find out the details on who this guy turned out to be when we got back. But my pit-bull partner was not leaving until he knew. I was so tired that I could hardly talk. I told him to call me. I was not even out of my uniform yet when I got paged to return to the cell area. The Identification officers had fingerprinted our guy first and were immediately rewarded with a fingerprint hit out of Alberta. Our drunk was wanted for attempted murder, and a Canada-wide warrant was in effect for his arrest. When the jig was up, the suspect admitted that he had gone to a graveyard in a small town, found a gravestone with the name of a child who had died shortly after birth, then applied for the identification he had shown us using that child's name.

You have to trust your instincts and be able to effectively articulate why you do what you do as a police officer. This guy was playing brinksmanship with us, telling us we would be sued for false arrest if we were wrong, and we very well could have been. Criminals often count on an officer's inexperience or fear of Internal Affairs to con their way out of trouble. Sadly, some officers will, as human nature dictates, take the easy way out. We could have ignored the drunk guy at the end of a very long night shift and hoped he made it home. We could have arrested him under the false identification and lodged him in the drunk tank, where he would have been released when sober with no consequences, free to roam.

So a little luck, trusting your instincts, and being thorough are a big part of any career. Being totally committed to the job at hand no matter how repetitive and routine the task could make all the difference in an outcome.

I got called down to the Major Crime section to join one of the K-9 officers to get a briefing on a suspect wanted for murder out of Regina. I looked at the picture of the woman and told them I knew where she was. It was one of the many benefits of working the same area for years—I had dealt with her son a couple of months earlier. What made him stand out in my mind was his intelligence in spite of some obvious fetal alcohol symptoms.

We went to the address and the son let us in. Our suspect was sleeping on a bare mattress laid out on the floor. She was co-operative and actually seemed relieved to be arrested, putting the first part of her ordeal to an end. After handcuffing her and advising her of her rights, I transported her to the Detention area of the Saskatoon police station. The K-9 officer, who was there in case the suspect ran, was a consummate professional at the scene—no high fives, just a casual wink to acknowledge an important arrest. The female special constable searched the suspect and in her pocket found a newspaper account of the murder from the Regina Leader Post. As well, there was a summary offence ticket that had been issued to her the previous day by two Saskatoon police officers for having open alcohol. The warrant for the murder was on the system when they wrote her that ticket. If they had checked, she would have already been in custody.

I tried never to tell this story to anyone above the rank of sergeant. The two officers were good cops. I used the story as a teaching point. Be thorough. You are well trained, well paid, and you have a duty to all of us to do your job to the best of your ability, every time.

One year I got paired up with a member who had just finished a colourful and productive turn in the Drug unit. He was a well-liked and respected officer. He was also a natural leader with an easygoing style who inspired confidence and loyalty. I had never left Patrol, and when he asked to work with me so I could show him the ropes, I was excited. Because I had not left the Patrol division, all the changes seemed to me to be a natural progression, but as my new partner told me, the changes were enormous. The technology and procedures had been adapting to new laws, new tactics, and the reality of doing more with less.

We had worked together many years before but only sporadically, when one or the other of our partners was absent. I followed his career after he left Patrol and was in awe at the arrests and undercover investigations he had engaged in. I knew that he and his partner were responsible for the decline in the availability of drugs during their time in the Drug section, particularly the illegally trafficked pharmaceutical opiates I had to deal with.

The violence and speed of Patrol—as opposed to investigations, with their surveillance, informants, and search warrants—are just a fact of policing. To be sure, the Drug unit faced many dangerous situations, especially undercover buys and high-risk search warrants. But in my mind, they were like bomber pilots: do the mission, and if you are not hurt, return to relative safety until the next mission. Patrol was the trenches: constant contact from the beginning until the end of every shift.

One night, we responded to a call at a smaller but notorious rooming house in the Riversdale neighbourhood of Saskatoon. It was probably built in the 1930s for transit workers. It was a long building with one- and two-bedroom apartments off a central hallway and two bathrooms for the residents to share. There was a door at each end of the hallway; the front one was glass so you could see all the way down the hallway to the back door, which was metal. We went to the source of the call, which was for loud music, and as I had been in this building many times before, the noisemaker agreed to shut it down. As we were preparing to leave, I heard a bang on the back door, as if someone was trying to get in. I opened it, and there was one of my regular morphine addicts trying to wrestle a mountain bike in the door. I knew that he did not have any outstanding warrants, so I reached down to grab the front wheel to give him a hand. He slapped my hand away. As I looked at his face, I realized he was high. His eyes were bulged, and he was sweating profusely. I thought to myself, maybe he did have a warrant I did not know about. He tried to push his way past my partner and me, and when I told him to hold up, one of the most intense and strangest struggles I had for years ensued.

I told him he was under arrest and tried to take him into custody. He was strong and covered in sweat. Between my partner and me and eventually a baton, we overpowered him into handcuffs. At the end of the struggle, as we were trying to catch our breath, my partner, who had missed the initial contact, asked what that was all about. I told him that I had tried to help the guy bring his bike in. "I had forgotten how much I missed Patrol," he replied. He later said the arrest was one of the toughest guys he had ever fought, and I agreed he was in the top 10. It turned out that the arrested man had missed court, but only he knew that because the warrant had not been placed in the system yet, and he was in possession of morphine.

My partner got promoted shortly after and went back to plainclothes. He, in my opinion, was one of the most imaginative and successful investigators the Saskatoon Police Service had during my career. To be honest and realistic, his talents were better utilized in investigations. But in his words, at least I got to show him a good time.

Patrol. It is a different kind of hunting. Absolutely addictive. *Source:* The StarPhoenix

10

CHECK YOUR EGO AT THE DOOR

IT IS SO EASY TO GET CAUGHT up in your work, no matter what your vocation, and to believe yours is the most important work occurring. The intensity of police officers' work contributes to this. You can run a gauntlet of emotions every day—frustration, anger, amusement, and all the other feelings—that all have to be kept in check until you finish your shift. There were times when I believed that no one else cared about what was going on, day after day, as long as it did not personally affect them. Your loyalty to the other officers in Patrol intensified because we alone did the same work and only we could appreciate it.

There is no one-shot prevention for this because it can happen several times over the course of your career. It is human nature to want to be valued or to value yourself sometimes more than you should. It doesn't just happen in policing or Patrol. No matter what you do, if you let your ego get away on you, it will reduce your effectiveness as a worker or a leader. I have caught myself a few times and have always regretted them. I made a sign for my desk in the Street Crimes unit, even though I was rarely there, that said "Working together effectively requires ego to be checked at the door."

I was on the train coming home from a holiday in Northern Ontario. I was in the bar car having a few beers with other passengers, just passing the time. Once the sun went down, the lights inside the railcar made looking out the window like looking in the mirror.

Trains are a very social place, and the conversation was lively. I was past the five-year mark in policing, and while there were some frustrations, I was having a lot of success and making some good solid arrests. One of the men told me he was a parole officer in Saskatoon. We started exchanging stories about people we knew and people we had dealt with. After about a half an hour, I was telling stories about parolees I had apprehended. He got up and left rather abruptly. I thought to myself, what an ignorant jerk, but when I looked at my reflection in the train window I realized that had been bragging, and that I was the ignorant one. Do not brag, just be.

Toward the end of a night shift, a call came in, a home invasion. A male victim had been severely injured. As the district sergeant, I raced to the call. Two constables were at the scene, doing their best to establish control until backup units arrived. I went to the injured male's location in the house. I knew from experience as soon as I saw him that his wounds were mortal and he would soon be dead. As DNA evidence and all the physical evidence could prove crucial to the homicide investigators, I did not want the crime scene contaminated more than it had to be. I told the firefighters who had arrived to assist the paramedics that they could not come in the house.

I have great respect and admiration for firefighters. Their need to save people is ingrained into their psyche and mindset, but in this case their physical presence was just more DNA and physical disruption in the crime scene. It is hard to explain this in thirty seconds at five-thirty in the morning to dedicated people just wanting to help, so I was abrupt and ran the call the way I thought it had to be run. I stayed at the scene until the Major Crime investigators took over. The injured male died.

When I returned to work, I was called into the divisional inspector's office to explain myself. The senior administration of the fire department wanted to know why I had kept the firefighters out of the crime scene. At first I was mad. Then I realized I was being arrogant. I automatically expected them to know my experience and respect my decision. The fact of the matter is, not everyone knows what you do or have done as a police officer. It applies to all trades or groups. People are doing their own jobs, and a story or two may reach them, but unless it is a very significant event, it is quickly forgotten. In policing, what one week is a priority event, the next week may be surpassed or overshadowed by the next calamity.

I explained to the inspector my observations at the scene and how I based my decisions on my experiences. Unfortunately, it was after my initial outburst of "Are you fucking serious?"

I made the mistake of assuming everyone knew or cared about what I did year after year. They could not, because they were doing their own thing. As leaders, you should know as much as you can about what your people are doing. Still, it is not possible to know it all. My explanation was required, and once I articulated what I had done, it was forwarded up the chain of command. I never heard another thing about it.

It was the start of a night shift, and after parade I headed out to my patrol car and found the gas tank was nearly empty. I went to the city yards to fill up, quietly bitching about the empty tank. While I was filling my patrol car, I heard a call of an accident with injuries at the far west end of the city come over the radio. I heard several officers volunteer to go and finished filling up the car. Accident-with-injury calls had become almost routine in the past couple of years as the city was growing and traffic volumes had increased accordingly.

I got back in my vehicle and started in the direction of the accident. I did not hit the lights and siren as I knew the first officers at scene would update Communications when they arrived, and driving through the early evening traffic at speed was always a dangerous undertaking. In about thirty seconds, I heard a female constable's voice on the radio. She spoke in a clear and understandable voice advising Communications that the accident was serious, asking for more units, saying children had been thrown from one of the vehicles and were lying on the roadway.

The stress and horror of what she was seeing was evident in the tone of her voice. Still, she was clear on what she needed and in control. My heart sank as I hit the siren. I radioed that I was en route and to keep the channel clear for the officer at the scene. The collision had taken place at one of the busiest intersections in the city, and traffic was heavy.

When I was within five hundred metres, I could see the overhead lights of police cars and fire trucks flashing in the night. Fortunately, there was a fire hall less than a mile from where the accident happened. Firefighters are a blessing at major accident scenes, with manpower, medical training, and large trucks to block traffic. While I was driving to the call, I could hear other units arriving at the scene. Anguish and frustration coloured their radio transmissions, then anger as one of the officers radioed that some of the occupants in one of the vehicles involved had fled on foot from the scene.

Another sergeant began to co-ordinate with the K-9 officer to try to locate these people. The scene of the accident and co-ordinating the response were my responsibility. Well-trained and experienced police officers can smoothly transition from one role to another if their on-scene supervisors are equally flexible. I knew I could not supervise the K-9 track or the investigation as it was unfolding, and even though I was the senior sergeant at the scene, I was confident that the other sergeants would do their jobs.

It appeared chaotic when I first got out my car, red and blue lights flashing over an unbelievable scene of a child's body crumpled on the road beside a damaged older North American car. Traffic was backed up as well, so the vehicle headlights illuminated blood on the roadway. Paramedics told me that with the assistance of the firefighters, they were going to do a "scoop and go" with the child on the road. Scoop and go is when first responders as quickly as possible stabilize, immobilize, and evacuate an injured person to a hospital because time was of the essence. The constable who arrived first told me what she knew as quickly as she could. I then told her to ride in the ambulance with the child's mother and another of the injured children to the hospital and to get as much information as she could there for the accident reconstruction team. I tried to make sure the officers had everything they needed to get the job done. The accident reconstruction team was called to attend, and in the meantime the scene had to be preserved as much as possible. Officers were assigned to get as many witness statements as they could from people who had stuck around. Surprisingly, there were more than usual, probably because there were children involved.

I taped the scene and listened as the K-9 track was being conducted. The K-9 officer tracks and an officer behind him calls in to Communications the direction they are going and any updates. Often, if the police dog is moving fast, it is a breathless narrative—K-9 officers tend to be in great physical condition and can go through more than one cover officer during a track. K-9 tracks are often switched over to another radio channel as well so the Communications staff have to monitor it separately.

The officer at the hospital updated us on the children's injuries, all of which sounded serious. There were three children in all. I stayed at the scene and waited for the accident reconstruction investigators. Vehicle records revealed who owned the vehicle the people had fled from, and he was picked up and taken in for a breathalyser test.

Once the scene-tape was up and traffic re-routed, there was nothing to do but wait for the accident reconstruction investigators to arrive. The criminal investigation was in someone else's hands. I called my wife because I knew this incident would be on the news and I was going to tell her I was all right. I got so choked up trying to talk to her, both of us knew I was not all right. In this case, trying to blunt the impact of instant news backfired on me, and I made my wife part of the trauma as well.

When the traffic investigators got there, I briefed them and wished them luck. The complexity of these investigations and the technical skills of these young officers in the reconstruction of incidents like these are astonishing. In the world of investigations, they do not get enough recognition for their skills. Every investigation is immediately high stakes because somebody almost always has been hurt or killed.

I went into the station and up to Detention to see how the criminal investigation was going. There was no light-hearted banter. The officers' grim faces reflected their anger, and the tension was palpable. The male in custody was in his twenties and was being ignorant to the officers who were dealing with him.

I should not have, but I said, "The children from this accident could die."

He replied, as cold as ice, "Not my fucking problem."

I was so angry I had to walk away before I did something that would jeopardize the investigation's outcome. As frustrated as I had been in a long time, I went to Central Records to tell the supervisor what to expect in the way of reports. Once again, I struggled to articulate the horror of the accident. The supervisor, whom I had known for years, let me vent and got her staff ready. I have written about the people who have to type the reports before, but again I have to say what a remarkable group of people support the officers on the streets.

The children survived. One of them had serious long-term injuries that would take her years to recover from. The mother was a single mother who had been contacted by the father of two of her children that evening. She was excited to have the children see their father and planned to make a night of it. Though she did not have a licence, she took the kids to McDonald's because she thought they deserved a break. In an old car without car seats and with no licence, she made choices she will probably always regret. People wanted to pass judgement on her choices, but in my opinion, she has suffered enough for her decisions.

As it was, the police were unable to prove who was driving the other car when the occupants fled or changed positions. The accident investigators were able to prove the registered owner had obstructed justice and he was convicted of that offence. He received a fine and no jail time. What the technicalities in law were that affected the outcome I do not know. I could not bring myself to read the whole report—it was too difficult. Even writing this story led to sleepless nights, tossing, turning, mumbling, and keeping my long-suffering wife awake with worry. For the mother and the children, I hope they have recovered and found a way to keep on living and growing. For everyone in the car who fled the scene and did not co-operate with the investigators, all I can say is that you failed your test as a person, and who or what did you beat?

The teamwork and professionalism of the paramedics, firefighters, and police at the scene of this challenging call, together with the citizens who stayed and stood witness, can get overlooked when weighed against the outcome. They all did, as they so often do, an outstanding job.

Teamwork works. Different priorities, same goals. *Source:* The StarPhoenix

11

ROBBERY

AT THE BEGINNING OF 2015, the chief of the Saskatoon Police Service, Clive Weighill, told the local paper that armed robberies were one of the crimes that saw a significant increase in 2014. Investigating robberies, armed or otherwise, is one of the least controversial aspects of police work. Everyone agrees robberies are crimes that need to be prosecuted. Almost everyone as a youth has played cops and robbers at one time or another, but real-life cops and robbers is high stakes and can be dangerous. Robberies are most often acts of desperation by addicts needing quick money. Sometimes they are gang related, either as a quick cash grab, an initiation, or to pay drug debts. There are thankfully very few armed robberies like you would see in the movies where the criminals plan their crime for years and use stop watches to execute a meticulous heist. With cell phones, in-progress armed robberies where a caller is on the phone as the robbery is happening are more and more common now.

One beautiful spring night toward the end of my career, we were just finishing our turnout parade for a night shift and were in the parking lot of the police station loading our cars. A call came in of an armed robbery in progress at a convenience store, not even four blocks away, from from a civilian calling it in on their cell phone from outside the window. The switch from preparation to action was instantaneous, and two constables and I were there and in the door in a minute, and the

87

suspect was in custody within another minute. I recognized the suspect, and he mumbled, "Sorry, Ernie." He had gone into the store with a small sword and attempted to rob it. Everything was caught on very high-quality surveillance video. It was possibly one of the quickest and most satisfying armed robbery investigations of my career—at least in the top 10.

I arrested a guy in November of 1999 on an outstanding warrant for theft under five thousand dollars. I knew he was an identified suspect from an armed robbery and that he was going to be charged. After telling him his rights, I advised him that the detectives would be coming to talk to him in regard to an armed robbery. I told him I had seen the surveillance video and I knew it was him. His reply? "I never used a weapon. Did you see a weapon?" If only it were always so easy.

A call came in of an armed robbery at a local restaurant just after 11 p.m., when the restaurant was due to close. Several units responded, including a K-9 officer. A search of the area came up empty. I told the constables that I would take the report and that they should keep hunting. I spoke to the badly shaken victim, and it took a few minutes to calm her down before she could provide a statement. She related that just before closing time, she had received a phone call asking what time the restaurant closed. She thought that it was strange, and for reasons that she could not explain, she saved the number.

A few moments later, a man armed with a large knife came in with his face covered and robbed her. Her clothing description was excellent, but saving the number was brilliant. I called the number from a blocked phone and asked a male who answered, "Where you at?" He asked, "Who is this?" and hung up. He did not answer the second call. Communications officers tracked down the number from local records. It turned out to be a cellular phone. A K-9 officer and I went to the subscriber's address.

A young woman, the subscriber to the phone, answered the door. She was genuinely surprised that we were at her address. She indicated that she had lent her phone to a friend who was not in the house right now. At this point, she became evasive and would not tell us the friend's name. We were strapped for manpower, so the K-9 officer volunteered to stick around the area in his unmarked car to see if her unnamed friend returned. Within an hour, a male glided out of the darkness on a bicycle and went into the house. We moved in quickly, not wanting to lose evidence. In the moment or two it took to get in the house, the suspect had geared down to his underwear and was pretending to be asleep. Unfortunately for him, his discarded clothing beside him was a perfect match to the victim's description. His jacket was unique, and it contained a knife. He was arrested in spite of his protestations of innocence.

During the preparation for the trial, the Crown prosecutor asked me to obtain the cell phone records related to the calls made on the night in question. I did not have a clue where to start, but one of the constables who had been present during the arrest volunteered. If I had drawn up the warrant, it would have delayed the trial, but he knew how to do it and in short order had it done. I realized how far I was falling behind in technical investigations and was glad for the help.

The accused maintained his innocence right up until he was convicted at trial. Then, in one of the many strange twists of our legal system, he was able to plead for leniency for the crime he had denied committing in the first place. He was sentenced to the penitentiary and then, upon his release, returned to Saskatoon, where he robbed a bank. He was arrested a couple of days later after some outstanding investigative work by detectives while in the process of robbing the same bank.

One night in October 2010, I was the acting staff sergeant when a call came in: an armed robbery had occurred on the east side of Saskatoon and shots had been fired. An alert citizen called in the licence plate number and vehicle description of the getaway vehicle. One of the patrol sergeants told officers not at the call to head for the bridges as the suspects were all wearing the colours associated to the Indian Posse street gang and they tended to be from the West Side. It was a good call because a moment later, the acting sergeant in Central Division who was paired up with a constable radioed in that he was behind the suspect vehicle. I had left the station and was in a marked car just blocks away. I got in behind the acting sergeant's patrol car, and we attempted to make a high-risk vehicle stop.

The suspects refused to stop, and a pursuit began. Although the speeds were not excessive, the suspect vehicle refused to pull over. As we went westbound past a warehouse, a Traffic officer, hidden perfectly, deployed stop sticks. He had not been on the air so I did not even know he was there. I am sure the suspects were equally surprised. The primary pursuit vehicle operated by the acting sergeant excitedly broadcast that the sticks had taken out two of the suspect vehicle's tires. The suspects turned onto a major street and continued on for eight more blocks before pulling into an alley in the Riversdale neighbourhood. The suspects, five in all, scrambled to get out of the vehicle and started to scatter. I saw a thin male exit out the front passenger-side door as that was the side I was on as I screeched to a stop. A large male came out of the back door on the passenger side, and the constable who had been riding with the acting sergeant tackled him. He tried to fight, but we quickly overwhelmed him, and he was handcuffed. It was very chaotic as the other suspects were being pursued in foot chases and everyone was snatching whatever air time they could to broadcast their progress. I secured our arrest in my patrol car and quickly advised him that he was under arrest for armed robbery and what his rights were. I went to take a look in the suspect's vehicle and saw loose crumpled money in the console and a handgun in a holster lying on the floor in front of the back seats.

Another sergeant said he believed that the driver had fled into a house, and along with him and four constables, we went there. The house was in darkness, but we could hear what sounded like a female yelling. We forced entry and started to clear the house. It was a large, three-storey house, and the registered owner of the vehicle was arrested on the second floor. A male on the third floor matched the description of the driver. He was lying on a bed, sweating profusely. He was arrested and handcuffed. As we were walking him out, he pointed to a pair of shoes that he said were his: black runners with red laces, which made sense if he was a gang member. They were seized.

One by one, K-9 officers and patrol members broadcast that they had arrests. In the end, all five suspects were in custody. I was absolutely pumped. I switched back to my in-command mode and assigned the acting sergeant, who was a senior constable, as the lead in the investigation. I delegated the role of exhibit officer to a young but very capable constable. I was completely confident in their abilities and went into the station to leave my reports. I did a media release and sent an e-mail to the detectives for follow-up investigation in the morning. I was proud of the team effort of the platoon members and proud of the citizens who had called in the vehicle information. No one had been hurt, even though several shots had been fired in the gas station they had robbed. Everything the detectives needed would be there in the morning when they came in. The gun and money had been recovered. The suspects were in custody waiting to be interviewed. All in all, I thought it was an outstanding example of good patrol work by motivated and dedicated officers. That is, until I came back to work.

I was called to task for not calling detectives to work the case from the outset. I tried to explain that detectives getting called in would only have resulted in half-awake investigators losing sleep as the majority of the bull work had been done. The next complaint was that I was using the detectives in a mop-up capacity. They resented it. The complaints were from the section supervisors; I never received any from the actual assigned investigators, so I do not know if the supervisors were moving their concerns forward or not. My version of teamwork apparently ruffled some feathers. But it did work: all five suspects pleaded guilty and received jail sentences ranging from eight years to one year. I would have done it exactly the same way if a situation like this had occurred again, but the criticisms took a little off the shine of the officers' achievements on that crazy night in October. We knew what we did.

Robberies, armed or otherwise, are violent and traumatic events for the victims. Personal space is invaded, and a person's sense of security is forever violated. An enormous amount of effort and investigation by detectives goes into identifying, arresting, and prosecuting robbers. Often, it is the work done by uniformed patrol officers arriving at scene that dictates how successful an investigation will be. Properly contained, crime scenes and immediate collection of witness information can make or break cases. Surveillance video never hurts either. Time is always of the essence, so when you see police driving at high rates of speed with lights and sirens going to a call, it is because the response is time sensitive.

Robbery investigations require teamwork and someone to take the lead. The lead can change, and the leadership transition should be as smooth as possible. From constable to patrol supervisor to forensic detective to detective, no-ego, no-nonsense transitions will be rewarded.

Share information without expectations. *Source:* The StarPhoenix

12

MEASURED RESPONSE

THERE ARE MANY SITUATIONS where your training provides the basic skills you need to deal with events you are called to deal with as a police officer. There are other situations where experience is the only teacher available.

Shortly after I started with the Saskatoon police service, I was dispatched to a call of an aggressive man handing out religious pamphlets in front of the Scotia Centre Mall in downtown Saskatoon. As I was approaching the area, I could hear my subject yelling and saw him thrusting pamphlets at people. Some tried to get by him with a hurried step, but he was relentless. It was three in the afternoon on a payday, so the downtown was packed. It was difficult to find a parking spot, so I just stopped behind some parked cars and put the overhead lights on.

What had started off as disturbance call would soon turn into a minor spectacle. I got out of my car and approached the man, who was in his fifties and solidly built. He ignored me, which is always a danger sign. I had to position myself physically in front of him before he would even acknowledge me. I told him that I had been dispatched in response to a civilian complaint about his aggressiveness and asked him to tone it down.

He told me that I could not interfere with the work of the Lord and turned away, thrusting his materials at people trying to pass by.

I came to the conclusion that this man was not operating at full mental capacity. He kept walking toward people, obviously frightening some of them with his aggression. They, of course, looked to me to do something about it. I put my hand on his elbow and he yelled, "Don't touch me! You have no right!" Now I was out of options, and I told him he was under arrest for causing a disturbance and went to take him into custody.

The fight was on. He grabbed one of my arms with a grip of steel and a to-and-fro ensued. I tried to get my arms free and his behind his back. He was so strong, I could not peel away his hands without him grabbing me somewhere else. Because he was older, I did not want to hit him to gain some distance, but it was coming to that.

People who would have been complaining about him previously were now yelling at me to leave him alone. All the while, the man was yelling for God to be his witness. Finally after a couple of strikes and punches, I got behind him and started to choke him out. Before he went unconscious, he surrendered. I handcuffed him while he kept yelling for people to watch what was happening.

A patrol sergeant arrived to transport him to Detention while I sorted myself out and tried to find witnesses. After a couple of minutes of people declining to give witness statements, frustrated, I jumped in my patrol car and went to the station. When I got to the Detention area, the man had not calmed down a lot and was preaching the Word to anyone who came by his cell.

I told him why he was arrested and advised him of his rights. He told me that God would be his judge. I asked him why he did not just tone it down like I had asked him to. He told me with the full righteousness of what he believed to be true, "You never said please."

It was another lesson about dealing with people suffering

from mental illness: sometimes the simplest things work. If I had asked him what it would have taken to make him less aggressive, I might have saved us both a few bruises.

On a beautiful summer day in 2006, I was on a day shift. The day had been relatively uneventful. People were moving around, shopping, and generally just enjoying the fine weather. I was heading west toward the liquor store on 20th Street to fly the flag as most of our daytime complaints originated there. Frequent patrols kept a lid on things. I saw a group of women pushing strollers and accompanied by other small children crossing the street on a walk light. There was an older pickup truck in front me approaching the red light. He was not speeding, but he was not braking either. The women screamed and moved out of the truck's path just in time as the truck drove through a solid red light. The driver had narrowly missed mowing down several women and children. Some swore and pointed at the truck. There was no need to—I had seen enough.

I hit the overhead lights and activated the siren. The driver carried on westbound, swerving in his lanes and making no attempt to stop. I was at this point in my career no fan of criminal pursuits, especially on day shifts. The dangers to everyone inherent in a chase were multiplied during the day. My heart was pounding as I called in that the driver was refusing to pull over. His speed was not excessive. As we approached another major intersection, once again the light was a solid red. No brake lights came on to show any attempt to stop. I hoped the siren was warning other drivers as the intersection was fairly open. We made it through without a collision. The truck was now driving in the oncoming traffic lanes.

I was considering ramming this obviously drunk driver as we

approached the next major intersection, which had blind corners from buildings. Southbound traffic would not see the lights or hear the siren until it was too late. All of a sudden, the truck appeared to lose power, rolled into some parking meters, and got hung up. I jumped out of my patrol car and yelled for the driver to shut off his vehicle. I went wide on the driver's side to get a look at him. He was slumped over.

I was furious. I thought, you son of a bitch, so drunk you passed out while driving! I ran up and pulled the keys out of the ignition as other officers pulled up. I could not smell any alcohol. I realized that the man I had wanted to jail a moment before was in medical distress. An ambulance arrived within minutes, and the man was transported to St Paul's Hospital only a couple of blocks away. Except for the paperwork and a letter to Saskatchewan Government Insurance and the Highway Traffic Board to have the man's licence reviewed, it was over. Some things are not the way they appear. What had looked blatantly criminal turned out to be poorly managed diabetes, and thankfully no one was hurt.

Defiance disorder was a relatively new psychiatric diagnosis to me in the last part of my career. I remember the first time I heard the term was when the staff sergeant was reading out the bulletins on a parade and it was included in the description of a missing person we were supposed to be on the lookout for.

In August 2013, I was asked to come to the river bank on Spadina Crescent in Saskatoon by constables who were assisting animal control officers apprehend a dog from some drunken people. It was a beautiful late summer night and the park was full of people of all ages. Citizens of Saskatoon love the river bank, and many people gather there with family and friends. The river bank in the summer is like a magnet to people who have for whatever reason turned their back on society. The mentally ill and addicted I expect to be there. People who have chosen to camp along the river and treat it as a place where the law doesn't apply are a different matter. There are young people who have chosen not to work and back pack across the country relying on other people's charity and goodwill. It is not illegal, and they certainly expect their rights to be respected. The problem for law enforcement is when they decide not to respect the rights of others or believe that the laws that govern the rest of us do not apply to them. It is one of those frequent situations that occur in policing: do nothing and be criticized, do something and look heavy-handed.

So there we were, dealing with four persons who fit the bill. All of them had been drinking and were very belligerent. The animal control officer calmly explained to them that the dog, a large mixed breed with a heavy tow chain for a leash, did not have tags or a licence. The dog was going to be seized and whoever owned it could come to the SPCA to claim it. A young woman I had never seen before began to physically obstruct the animal control officer, a law enforcement official, by refusing to release the chain and trying to pull the animal away.

The woman was dressed in old army clothes with pins and slogans all over them. I warned her to step back and let go of the dog. She appeared to be drunk enough that she would keep causing problems if left on her own, so I arrested her for public intoxication, a non-fine, non-criminal charge, so that she did not end up escalating her behaviour and getting herself into criminal charges. She protested, and said that if she were drunk she would have head-butted me. She began screaming and swearing as I escorted her up the river bank. I asked her to settle down as her antics were attracting a crowd, including children. This made her even worse. She started yelling about Saskatoon being a hick town and how she could not wait to get out of here. I quietly her told it could not be soon enough. All the way to Detention, she ranted about how people should just live free and how the police had no reason to interfere with her life.

When we got to the elevator to go up to the Detention area, she went limp and said I would have to drag her upstairs. I had seen this tactic a hundred times before, and it gets old real quick. Surprisingly, age, gender, and prior history have nothing to do with who will try it. I stayed put until two officers came to give me a hand lifting her without hurting her. Once we got her upstairs, she was unhandcuffed. She was told to put her hands on the counter so she could be searched by a female officer. She replied, "Everywhere else they make you put your hands on your head." It was obviously not her first rodeo.

She became increasingly agitated and aggressively tried to bait us into using force to make her comply. Finally, I had had enough. We took control of her arms and took her to a cell. As we turned to step away, she spat in the face of the Detention sergeant. She then took off her brassiere and said she was going to hang herself.

The Public Order Unit has the equipment and specialized training to safely restrain a violent and suicidal person, so members on duty were called, and after being briefed, they went into the cell. The woman was placed in a restraint chair. It looks inhumane, and it is never pretty, but the alternative was unthinkable.

Was this young woman mentally ill or nastily narcissistic? This scenario plays out frequently in all police jurisdictions. All too often, it is where mental health issues and the police's need to enforce laws meet.

At the start of a Thursday night shift in the beginning of August 2013, I had just left the station and was heading westbound on 22nd Street West when my cell phone rang. I pulled off the street and turned into a lane on the north side of 22nd. I was just about to answer the phone when I looked up and saw a young woman running toward me, waving her arms to get my attention. She appeared to be running from a car parked a block further west in the lane.

I drove toward the car, and as I pulled up and started to get out, a male ran southbound across 22nd Street, narrowly missing getting hit by the heavy, fast-moving traffic. A second male, shirtless, was by the passenger side of the car and had a large knife tucked into the front of his waistband. The woman who had run toward my patrol car and another woman who had been on the passenger side front seat exited the driver's side and said the man with the knife had tried to stab them.

The man with the knife said the woman tried to stab him. Decision time. The man with the knife was only about three metres away from me, so he was the primary threat. I pulled my pistol and ordered him to the ground. I was thankful that he complied. I quickly handcuffed and disarmed him. I still did not know what was going on. I called for additional units and put the man in my car. Once he was off the ground, I realized the man was actually a boy, fifteen years old probably. As soon as he started talking, I realized that his voice had not even dropped yet. Judging by the smell and his speech, he was also drunk.

Officers arrived quickly, and we began to get the story from the women. The youth in custody and the unidentified male who had run away had robbed another youth at a convenience store moments earlier. The women saw the robbery and were slowly following the suspects in their car. They were just about to call the police when the suspects turned on them. They were too close for the women to back away in time. The young man had tried to stab them, and both threatened to kill them. The women provided statements to the other officers.

Now that I knew what charges I had, I went back and arrested the kid in my car for two counts of assault with a weapon, possession of a weapon dangerous to the public peace, and threats to cause death. I advised him of his rights and asked if he wanted a lawyer. He refused to acknowledge his rights at first and said he just wanted to go to jail so he could go to sleep. I told him his rights again, and it seemed like whatever adrenaline high he was on had left him and he realized he was in trouble. Still he said he did not want to call a lawyer. After I ran his name through the system, he came back as previously charged for assault and out on an undertaking with conditions not to drink.

His age was confirmed as fifteen and he refused to name who he was with. Other officers went looking for the youth who had been robbed in the first place. He was never located and never came forward with a complaint. The women were not hurt. As I was talking to them, they repeatedly told me they were sick of street robberies and that is why they had followed the suspects.

I transported the youth to Detention. The heat of the moment had passed, and I was so very glad he had hit the ground when I told him to. Shooting someone, especially a youth, was not the way I wanted to end my career. After he was in the cells, I went to notify his parents of the arrest. His father was a long-time gang member, and no one would tell me where he could be found. I told an aunt and knew someone would pass on the information. The whole incident was incredibly sad: the women who tried to do the right thing and became victims themselves. A fifteen-year-old drunk, brandishing a knife and robbing people. No one wanting to tell me where his father was and never getting a phone call from him to find out what had happened. At the end of the day, just because the work was difficult or sad, you could never walk away from it while you were there.

13

No Pretty Woman Scenario

BACK IN THE 1980s, several unsolved murders were linked to the activities at 20th Street West and Avenue B South. Prostitutes openly used to work that corner and the corner of 3rd Avenue and 20th Street East. I could not understand as a constable why these places were allowed to flourish as everyone, especially the police, knew these were major hubs of criminal activity. I do not think the present model of the Saskatoon Police Service would tolerate such activity. But like all things, the skills and will to do something have to be learned as well as driven by public concern.

I do not think the police service had the energy after the so-called Hooker Wars in the mid-eighties. The Hooker Wars were a series of murders and shootings that had occurred in a struggle to take control of the prostitution and drug trade in Saskatoon before I had started with the Saskatoon police. Sometimes I suspected that because the crimes and activity were well known, it was better to have it be where you knew it was rather than spread throughout the city.

Recently, prostitution has been in the news. It has been subject of many debates after the Supreme Court struck down the current prostitution laws. The people who challenged the laws had their own agendas. They cleverly used the issue of the safety of women involved in high-risk behaviour so that they can legitimize and normalize an ongoing criminal enterprise. The only beneficiaries are organized crime.

There is no "Pretty Woman" scenario in prostitution. Pretty Woman was a movie that portrayed a beautiful woman who was a prostitute that found love and happiness with a handsome, rich customer. Prostitution is one of the most exploitive human interactions. The term "sex trade workers" infuriates me, as if they had applied for a job, and after vigorous screening and training, they are employees entering into an acceptable vocation. The reality is quite different. Prostitution, especially street prostitution, is a dirty, dangerous world, and in many respects an extension of the vilest forms of sexism and racism left for the most part unchallenged and unresolved in our country.

Over the course of my career, I dealt with prostitution and its aftermath almost every day and night I was working. A sad fact of my police career is that the overwhelming majority of prostitutes in the area I worked were Native. I'm sure it will anger some people when I say this, but it was a fact. I cannot deny or sugar-coat it, because every day and every night they were there for everyone to see. The women in my district were among the most victimized segments of Canadian society I have ever seen. The pimps were the most ruthless and cruel, the johns the most pitiful and sometimes the most aggressive. No value was placed on the women's dignity.

They were considered a commodity, but they are not just commodities. They are mothers, sisters, and daughters of someone. They come from somewhere, and they have a story. To me, all the talk of laws, rights, and inquiries seems to depersonalize them even more. The choice to start selling themselves may not have been entirely theirs, but the choice to get out will ultimately be. Helping make that happen would be money well spent.

Sadly, street prostitution does not only affect the people doing it. It affects the neighbourhood as well. Kids have to be told to look out for discarded needles in their yards and in the parks where they play. Prostitutes work in the day, and children have to pass by scantily clad and often high women on the way to school. Even more tragic is that some of the kids may even be related to the girls and women out there working. Johns will proposition anyone, whether they are a prostitute or not. It has to be disheartening if you are a thirteen-year-old kid going to school and some man trolls by you because you are a Native girl.

It is a quality-of-life issue. The high use of medical facilities by street workers affects people in the community's ability to access doctors. People should not have to be forced to watch this day after day and night after night simply because they live in a poorer neighbourhood.

The longer the women worked, the deeper their addictions became, and the harder their outlook became, if they made it that far. Many died violently, but many, many more died of overdoses, suicides, and broken health. Thirty-year-old women looked sixty, thin, haggard, and scarred, with little or no light behind their eyes.

Prostitution became multi-generational. One mother, herself a grizzled veteran of the street sex trade, forced all her daughters onto the street to make more money for drugs and to enable her to turn fewer tricks. All three daughters were from different fathers. All of them, however, had their mother's look. Their mother, who must have been a beautiful young woman, passed on her beauty. When I first started patrolling Riversdale, they were young, just over eighteen. I used to street-check them constantly and would stop any john who circled the area or stopped to talk to them.

Their mother hated me with a passion. Her years on the street, I believe, made her hard enough to be capable of any violence. She had enough of her language to curse me roundly in Cree. Over the course of the next few years, the oldest daughter, who in any other life could have been a teacher or even a model, became hopelessly addicted to IV drugs. Ts and Rs—Talwin and Ritalin—were the most common drugs, referred to on the streets as a poor man's cocaine. Her beauty faded, but she was very much in demand, both as a commodity to her mother and as a prostitute. She always had a kindness and a sadness in her eyes that you could see, even when I arrested her on outstanding warrants or for violations of the many court orders she received over the years. She never displayed the deep-seated hatred her mother so freely dispensed, but her loyalty to her mother never flagged either. I could not understand it and still don't. She eventually overdosed as her fixing became more erratic and her recklessness with dosages got the better of her.

The middle daughter was the same. She hooked up with the most dangerous men and was assaulted so many times, I lost count. Still, she would smile when I arrested her, seemingly almost glad for the break from the streets, and she could always blame me for her forced absence. In spite of all my efforts, she would not turn on those who used her. Eventually, she was arrested on outstanding warrants and she was in possession of drugs, resulting in more charges. Her health had deteriorated so badly that she was sent to the hospital from the Saskatoon Police Service Detention area. Once, at the hospital, she escaped, and after she was recaptured she was sent to Pine Grove, a woman's correctional centre in Prince Albert, Saskatchewan, where she died.

The girl's mother died shortly afterward. I was not at the call, so I do not know all the circumstances.

The youngest daughter kept working the streets. There was no animosity between us. I would arrest her if she needed to be arrested, but it was like there was an unspoken understanding between us. The tragedy of their lives needed no words. I did not need to say that I understood or ask if I could help because I knew she would say no. She had gone to part-time prostitution when I retired and seemed to have her addictions under control.

There is no pretty woman scenario in prostitution, nor will there ever be. So, whose responsibility is it to stop this kind of exploitation? Ultimately, it is all of ours. But first and foremost, it is the women themselves who need to take the first step. I cannot imagine, however, that a young woman arrives at the decision to walk out the door and sell herself to a stranger on her own. There has to have been some life-changing event before someone takes the drastic step into the abyss of street prostitution. Sexual abuse, incest, drug addiction, desperation for money, low or no self-esteem, somebody willing to take advantage of them, or a combination of all of these are the most common factors in a woman's decision to sell herself.

By default, police become their protectors and are the first ones to be criticized when something happens to them. Once again by default, police have to be the most creative in offering solutions. Sadly, we will never eradicate street prostitution, but society needs to speak openly about it. We can let young women know that no situation or state of affairs is so complete that they have to resort to prostitution. There is always someone who is willing to help or show you a different way.

When I told one of my former colleagues that I was writing a chapter about prostitution, she told me that she had enjoyed her time in the Vice unit and had dealt extensively with prostitutes and the men who used them. She said that she missed the girls the most. They were super manipulative sometimes, but they all had a story. The more she dealt with them, the more she felt charged with their safety and well-being. As she was talking, her feelings for the women were clear—a genuine understanding and empathy for the human beings caught in a cycle of exploitation. As she was talking, I could see she was back there, working Vice. This is a common phenomenon for police when they recount their experiences. The hyper-vigilance was in her eyes. There are a lot of dangerous, sick men out there and desperate, sometimes dangerous women who interact every night.

One late-summer evening a couple of years after I started, I was patrolling by a church on 20th Street. I was working alone because we didn't pair up until 11 p.m. in the early part my career. I saw woman in her forties get out of a car as I rounded the corner. She had a young girl with her, about four years old, dressed in a white dress fancy enough for a wedding. What I was seeing did not sink in until the woman disappeared between two houses with the child in tow. I was instantly outraged and stopped the car the woman had got out of as he tried to drive away. The driver was an older man in his late sixties or early seventies by his appearance. It became so obvious to me what I had just stumbled upon, I dispensed with any professionalism and asked him point-blank if he was going to buy the little girl. I was shaking and seething with anger. I knew I was looking at a pedophile. I cursed my lack of experience because the woman had gotten away, and now I was seized by this traffic stop.

He had no outstanding warrants and his registration and licence were in order. He could have been anyone's grandfather. I threatened that if I ever saw him in the area again, something would happen him that he could not even begin to comprehend. A hollow and empty swing of frustration is what it amounted to. I had thought that I was switched on by this point in my career. I had thought wrong. I had lots to learn about the levels of depravity people would sink to and the pure evil people are capable of. I never saw him, the woman, or little girl again except in my mind. Whenever I thought I had learned everything about policing the streets, I would think about this incident and realize that I could always learn more. Sometimes, what you see can be so far from your belief system that it takes a minute to realize what you're seeing. In this case, it was a moment too long.

Late one night, I was on the stroll. In Saskatoon, the stroll is a generic term used for an area where street prostitution most frequently occurs. The courts in Saskatoon clearly spelled out streets and avenues as the borders when prohibiting offenders from entering into the area during certain hours in an attempt to curtail the activity. I saw a brown van parked and running on a residential street behind a hospital. Given the night-time activities, the hour, and the fact that I had never seen this van in the area before, I hit the overhead lights and pulled in behind it. As soon as I hit the lights, the oldest of the three sisters I spoke about earlier opened the passenger side door and ran. She looked terrified. I could not see injuries and I knew who she was, so I knew I could always catch up to her after I was done dealing with the driver. I approached the driver. He was about thirty years old. His van was obviously a work vehicle, a late seventies General Motors product. As I shone my flashlight into the interior, I saw a three-foot length of thick yellow nylon rope between the seats. I asked the driver for his licence and registration. I could see he was nervous, and he looked like he had been and caught in the middle of something. He had the look of a predator that had lost his prey. His reactions were out of proportion to a regular john caught with a prostitute.

I obtained all of his documents and began to question him regarding the woman. He was evasive and overly polite. He had no warrants or outstanding issues with the courts. He did not protest when I seized length of rope. Aside from the nagging suspicion that I was dealing with a very sick and twisted man, I had nothing. I had to let him go. Unbelievably, the woman who had fled the vehicle was back on the stroll within a couple of hours. I stopped and asked her what had happened to make her run from the vehicle. She said she did not want to talk about it and that it was okay. No amount of appeals to her safety and for the safety of the other girls out there could get her to tell me what had happened to make an experienced prostitute like her flee in terror from the van. I did not know what to make of it, so I completed a street-check log and entered all the event's information into a national database, including the scenario of how the contact had occurred. I kept the piece of rope for years, right up until I retired, because you just never know.

The caravans of men who came into the area from the suburbs or small towns around Saskatoon were a contemptible and loathsome lot. I stopped them all the time, listening to the same stories: I'm in town looking for my friend. I was in town to look for a car that was for sale. I am here on business. I couldn't sleep so I decide to drive around. My questioning was equally sarcastic: Oh, you had to come to a high prostitution area at three o'clock in the morning as there is no other place you can drive around. Who is your friend? Where does he live? I detested their weakness as men. Some of them caused me to truly fear for the women and girls because of their obvious lack of empathy and their barely concealed capacity to cause pain. Still, if you did not catch them in the act, you were powerless under the laws as they existed at the time. Every once in a while, I would get lucky and they would be impaired or have weapons and drugs so I could arrest them. But realistically, I was just getting the slow, the weak, and the stupid.

They will never stop coming until there is no reason to come. A terrible and tragic circle of supply and demand, with women of all ages as the currency, will go on until it becomes socially unacceptable.

"If I have to come back here again, it will not be good." *Source:* The StarPhoenix

14

INQUIRY?

THE CALL FOR A NATIONAL INQUIRY into missing and murdered Indigenous woman is everywhere in the media as I am writing this. By the time you read this, maybe one will have been called by the government.

The amount of violence against all women I have seen in my career is staggering. At this point, in my opinion, this is not a national issue; each and every case is a local issue and a local investigation. Each and every woman or girl who is missing or whose murder is unsolved is the responsibility of the police who have jurisdiction and the community where the victim is from. This is the simple truth in Canada of criminal acts and their investigations. Short of creating a national task force to do these investigations, this is how they will be done for the foreseeable future. Even if a national task force were formed, it would be years before it was effective, as every case would have to be revisited, and by the time the mechanics were figured out, much ground would be lost. Calling an inquiry would buy time for everyone who should be taking a lead and providing a solution. Time is the enemy of any open murder or missing person's case being investigated. The leads and solvability grow colder every day that we just talk.

The term "high-risk lifestyle" has been used to describe the some of the victim's pre-murder behaviour. The outcome would seem unavoidable as sometimes some of the victims' lifestyles were extremely high risk. When an extreme sports athlete is killed, however, most of us do not classify them as living a high-risk lifestyle. We do not try to move some of the blame to the victim. Instead, we call them adventurous or free-spirited. But we consistently do this with women who are murdered. In reality, the term "high-risk lifestyle" just diminishes the impact of the murder on the sensibilities of the community. Putting values on a victim doesn't change the fact that they were the victim of a violent act. In many cases of other pre-murder or assault behaviour, the only risk factor was being an Indigenous woman.

The women and girls are not numbers to bolster each group's argument for or against an inquiry. They are people with families who deserve answers to where they are or how they came to be where they were found. Case by case, investigation by investigation is the only way this will truly get done. The strength of each investigation depends on any number of things: the training and skill of the assigned investigators, the co-operation of the community, and the evidence available. These will, in the end, provide the only real answers.

There is no quick and easy fix to these cases. No inquiry, no matter how far-reaching or in-depth, will solve individual cases. It comes down to police work, co-operation of witnesses, and evidence. There will be missed clues and opportunities. There will continue to be investigations that fall short of the mark. There will be suspects who maintain their silence and who don't co-operate.

In the early nineties, I took a call from a teenage girl I had known since I started with the Saskatoon police. She was involved in the solvent-sniffing crowd when I first met her, but she turned it around on her own. She was a troubled kid with a great attitude and a big smile. Her promise was always that she would do better. On the phone, she was clearly upset and told me that two men had invited her to an apartment. Once they had her there, they had used markers to paint on her breasts. She knew one of the men by name. The second man terrified her, and she was so agitated she would not even begin to describe him. The complainant was a good kid making bad choices, but I believed her. I knew the man she named, and after getting a statement, I went to his apartment and arrested him for sexual interference. He was unrepentant and asked why I believed the complainant, whom he called a lying little cunt. I was unable to get the second suspect identified, but I did not give it much thought because there was so much going on at the time.

The matter never came to trial, or at least I never received a court notice. My complainant had gone missing, but no one ever told me. It was not until the bodies of three women and a teenager were found on a golf course outside of Saskatoon that I found out where this girl was. My sergeant told me the names of the victims and asked if I knew them. I told him I did, and I cannot describe the sadness I felt and still feel. She had been murdered by a serial killer, John Crawford. The man I charged was his buddy. If I had been more persistent with the girl, I suspect the second man who had sexually interfered with her would have been identified as Crawford. It will always be one of those situations where you will never know what could have happened. It was a relatively minor sexual assault charge, but it could have been enough to stop Crawford from murdering those other women.

I do not know, and I will never know. I do know that I had no malicious motive or intent to miss such an opportunity. An inquiry would find many missed opportunities and human errors in investigations at its completion many years from now. It could also assign blame or make for better investigations. It also may divide us even further on racial lines and lead to much more discord.

In the end, though, it is about victims and perpetrators. Whatever the motive, whatever the crime, racist sexual predators, pimps, and gangs keeping women in check, partner violence, or an "opportunity" sexual assault and murder of a vulnerable woman, the perpetrators need to be brought to account. No inquiry, short of giving a sordid and tragic overview of all 1,200-plus cases, will ever bring them to justice and give the families any closure.

An inquiry would cost untold millions of dollars. The Pickton trial and inquiry cost over one hundred million dollars, and no one seemed satisfied with the results. A national inquiry would easily cost ten times that, and it would require witnesses to come to it or it would have to go to them. Money should not be the determining factor, but it is something to consider. Would it not be better spent providing education, shelter, and training to those at risk and those who are charged with their protection?

True leadership by everyone involved is what is needed. Realistic expectations need to be presented and action taken now. If a woman asks for help, it should be available. If a working police officer is approached by someone wanting help, the officer should be able to steer them in a clear direction. Action, real and visible, is what will end the disproportionate victimization of Indigenous women. Case by difficult case, investigation by investigation, there is no easy way to do this, national inquiry or not.

My own experience with inquiries is what I am drawing from. The Stonechild inquiry actually was the catalyst for many positive changes in Saskatchewan between the First Nations and police services. Though by no means perfect, the relationship has improved tremendously from where it was. It was one case, and the inquiry cost twenty million dollars.

During the inquiry, there were many side issues, motions, and requests for standing. A national inquiry would be unwieldy as every group clamoured for standing and to be heard to advance their own particular agenda. The names of the missing and murdered women and girls would be lost in the ensuing process, with no answers and no satisfaction for years for the families. In the end, solid recommendations and policy might emerge as findings. Things might change for the better, but it would be years from now. Lawyers and their support staff will not be doing all of this for free. Witnesses and experts will require compensation, and all the while, the situation of Indigenous women and girls will not be improving.

We know what is required. It is leadership. Leadership at every level. The call for a national inquiry seems to have given us all tunnel vision. The current federal government has become the whipping boy, but there were many governments before this one who provided the same kind of anaemic leadership on the issue. Shame and blame abound but do nothing to change anything. Governments seem to spend more energy trying to justify not doing anything than actually doing anything. We expend enormous energy and craft clever prose trying to establish our respective positions on where we stand on this.

In the end, from my perspective, it is the families of the missing and murdered women who are important, and all the resources that are available should be focused on them, finding answers and justice if they can be found. The hard, inescapable fact that it will take determined police and co-operating witnesses to find answers often gets overlooked, as do the undeniable successes of these efforts. Everything else, while well intended, is just rhetoric.

I do not know what the current state of each individual investigation underway is, or the status of each case. Somebody does, and an update or a request for public assistance on each case by the responsible police agency might raise the awareness even more than the endless debate over a national inquiry. Police are by default in many ways community leaders, and detailed accounting seems like a good place to start. They will, of course, have to weather the storm that will accompany a frank accounting. They are used to that.

Multi-tasking; everyone wants and needs information. *Source:* The StarPhoenix

15

NOSEY NEIGHBOURS

I WAS AT A MEETING IN LATE 2014 and met a woman who told me that the first time she saw me was when she was working at Scotiabank and I was trying to arrest a man just outside her window. To her, it was obviously not going as planned for me. She asked her co-worker if they should call the police and then had a laugh because I was the police. She remembered the man and the incident. Nothing goes unnoticed, which is sometimes a good thing to keep in mind for everyone.

If you are a police officer, you should never discount or undervalue the power of observant (or downright nosey) neighbours. They often do not want to get directly involved, but they will talk over their fences or make comments as they are pushing their garbage bin to the curb. Sometimes they are just gossipers, and other times they will throw an investigative gem your way that leads to a break in a case or an arrest that could not have happened without them.

Always take a minute to listen if you can. Over the years, I received many calls from informants telling me that they had tried to tell police at a crime scene where the suspect had fled or where the evidence had been dumped, only to be dismissed by an officer in a hurry. There is a fine line between getting distracted by someone who just wants to comment or complain and getting real timely information. Experience will help sort out information more quickly and accurately. Unless there is an immediate threat, you get the experience by listening. If you have lost sight of your suspects for more than a minute, stopping for ten seconds to listen might make all the difference in a successful apprehension.

Informants to the police, whatever their motive, have put their well-being in the hands of the officer who has received and acted on the information. Some officers and the most successful investigators actively seek informants. This is one the most fruitful and perilous areas of policing. Having someone on the inside is the ultimate investigative technique. I never got to that level because I stayed in Patrol pretty much my whole career, and some informants are very needy and have no schedule. The informants I had were people I had pitched to about the safety of their community. Even if they were involved in criminality, I asked them to call me if they saw something they knew would hurt everybody, and they did.

One of the best informants I ever had was a woman. She has passed away, so telling her story will not put her in any danger. This woman was a heavy drinker, passing out in so many different locations that she was kind of a local legend with the beat cops at the time. She was a tiny woman with classic Dene features, high cheekbones, and dark-skinned. The woman had a sense of humour, and she was self-effacing, with a big heart. She was almost invisible. Posing no threat to anyone but herself, she used to pass out in all temperatures. She would take shelter in garbage disposal bins, air intakes, doorways, and under vehicles.

The first time I dealt with her, she was in a garbage bin. I got her out and wondered how this slight, middle-aged woman could find herself in such circumstances. She was embarrassed because she had wet herself and apologized for having to sit in my car. I told her not to worry about it. I explained that I was going to have to take her to the drunk tank so that she would be safe and warm. She told me that would be fine and that she liked the way I was treating her. To think anyone could be mean or rude to such a woman upset me a little. She told me that she did not like smarty-pants cops. "Smarty pants" is one of those terms I often heard from middle-aged Native people growing up. I do not know why it was so popular; it just was.

As I was driving her into the station, to my surprise she told me where a wanted suspect was staying. She told me his routes and routines, when he moved around, and who his girlfriend was. She said he was wanted for a sexual assault, and everyone on the street was afraid of him. This woman told me how to knock on the door so he would answer without even looking to see who was there. After she was lodged in cells, I did some quick checks on the computer, and sure enough, the suspect was wanted. He had an outstanding warrant for sexual assault, requested after the detective investigating was unable to track him down. Her degree of accuracy was astonishing—it was almost like she had written the report. People on the street talk about crimes, even if it is to each other and not to the police. Within an hour, another constable and I had this male in custody. I went back to her cell to tell her, but she was sound asleep.

Our relationship lasted almost ten years. She would occasionally sober up and go home, back up north, for a few months. Inevitably, she would come back to Saskatoon, where she would become visible and invisible at the same time. She gave up wanted suspects whose offences offended her sense of right and wrong. Sexual and domestic assaults and street robberies, she knew what was going on. She would have been a great street cop or undercover operator.

This kind and sad woman would take nothing in return, not even coffee or cigarettes and certainly not cash. The only thing she asked was that I did not become a smarty-pants cop. Sadly, she was determined to drink herself to death, and eventually she did. I took the call from an older gentleman who had let her stay at his place for a few days so he would not have to be alone. She died in her sleep and thankfully in a bed, not even fifty-five years old.

When people see a crime in progress and an officer involved in a struggle to take someone into custody, their reactions are as unique as they are. Some are shocked and do nothing. Some will record the incident on their phones. Others will call the police in case the other police are not aware. Sadly, there are some people who will scream support for the criminal fighting with the police and encourage to the criminal to escape. Then there are those people who will actively assist the officer to take the suspect into custody. In the vast majority of physical encounters, the police have it under control, but there were times when a citizen's help made all the difference in the outcome of a violent arrest.

Early in my career, I was in the downtown area by an old hotel called the Windsor when I saw a guy with an outstanding warrant for theft. I got out of my patrol car and arrested him. He was mouthy but compliant as I handcuffed him. As I was putting him in the car, another man ran up with blood pouring out of his mouth and pointed at a guy coming of the doorway of the hotel. He said, "That guy just robbed me." The alleged robber had not seen me until the victim had yelled. As soon as he did, he started to run toward a mall. After a short foot pursuit, I tackled him. The situation had unfolded so quickly that my last radio transmission was that I had the first suspect in custody and I was 10-4. The robbery suspect was bigger, stronger, and more desperate than I had anticipated. I was quickly losing the advantage I had when I had tackled him as he struggled to get up. I could not get his arms under control and into handcuffs. My back was to the bar and I did not know if he had any accomplices. Then I heard a deep booming voice behind me: "Do you need a hand?"

I looked and saw a young man and woman obviously out on a date. The young fellow was big and appeared athletic. He was almost a stereotypical strapping young farmer, right down to the cowboy boots. I asked if he could grab an arm on the suspect, which he did, and the two of us quickly powered him into handcuffs. I was catching my breath when he asked, "You good?" I told him yes and thanked him. The woman said, "We are going to be late for the movie," and with a nod they were gone. I never got his name, and though it has been many years since, I just want to say thanks again.

Believe it or not, there was a criminal charge founded in English common law and carried over to the criminal codes of many jurisdictions, including Canada, for failing to assist a constable who requests assistance. It is very rarely enforced—I never saw the charge used in Saskatoon over the course of my career. The wording was interesting, and there was a safeguard in the section so a constable could not get someone to do their work for them and had to be in real need of assistance.

Times have changed since the law was drafted. There is no cut-and-dried response to what you should do if you see an officer in trouble. You have to let your own moral compass guide you. If you cannot physically help, be a witness, record it if you can, and keep a safe distance—in my experience, criminals do not want impartial witnesses. If they know you are there, sometimes just your presence is enough to stop them.

There were many times over my career where people helped me in tough situations without regard for their own safety. I was always thankful, and it always reinforced my belief in the basic goodness of people.

16

NO WARRIORS HERE

I RECENTLY WATCHED a documentary on street gangs in Winnipeg, in particular Native street gangs, featuring the Manitoba Warriors, Crazy Cree, and the Indian Posse. The theme was to show how past wrongs done against Native people led them to the gangs and were a legitimate justification for the gangs.

Almost every nation has been the victim of some traumatic event in its history, be it war, famine, disease, or any of the other Seven Horsemen. The ability to recover and move forward is what makes a nation successful and ultimately stronger. Nearly everyone in Canada can point to an injustice done to their forebears at some point in their history. In Canada, moving forward is easier, and it can be done without fear of being murdered for the effort, as happens in many other parts of the world. If we respect and learn from our past, there is no direction other than forward.

Even while presenting this theme in the documentary, the main gang member they were interviewing pulled the plug on the bath by repeatedly saying gang life was all about the money. So there it was, gangs are all about the money. No noble resistance or effort to improve the life of other Native people. No connection to our culture as Natives except the names of the gangs. It is like the old practice of hiring men of Mediterranean descent to play Indians in the old movies—no authenticity there.

I policed gangs in my career, and where I worked meant most of the gang members were Native. In Saskatoon, the gangs were the Indian Posse, the Native Syndicate, Crazy Cree, Red Scorpions, and Saskatchewan Warriors. A large mixed-race gang called Terror Squad and a couple of all-female gangs with names like the West Side Queens rounded out the street gang picture. More gangs were appearing in Saskatoon in the last years of my career, almost all of them trying to muscle in on the drug trade as our economy flourished, but they were out-of-province gangs.

There were fighters and some ultra-violent people in these gangs, but not a warrior in the true sense of the word among them. Every First Nation in Canada has a defined role through their traditions of what a warrior is and what his or her responsibilities are and were. The central theme is to protect the people. Not one gang member I ever dealt with came even close to being a warrior. They dealt drugs, pimped women, intimidated elders, and meted out violence as a fore- and afterthought. They contributed to most of Saskatoon's murders in the past ten years and have tortured people over drug or turf disputes. The bandanas and gang signs were all imported from the south. Their music, gestures, and language were all hijacked from other gangs. Even the graffiti scrawled across most inner-city neighbourhoods was crude and did nothing to make people see them as protectors.

A triple shooting caused the Saskatoon Police to form the Street Crime unit in 2003. The unit was created to deal with the street gangs who had become firmly entrenched in Saskatoon during the years the Saskatoon Police Service was mired in controversy and under scrutiny. I was on days off when the shootings happened and was still in Patrol. The detectives had developed suspects and had arrest warrants issued by the time I returned to duty.

I knew all the wanted suspects from previous arrests, but one of them surprised me. I knew him as a well-spoken, intelligent young man. I had no idea he had slipped into the gang life. He had committed crimes before, but always for his own purposes and not for a gang. Most of the time, he had been drinking or high when he had broken the law. It was no excuse though, and he was always remorseful.

I had been with my partner a couple of years by this time. A big guy from a farming background with a deep booming voice, he loved police work and had no love for criminals. He was very intelligent and insightful, and I trusted him in every situation. We were of like mind when it came to police work: you had to be out there to catch criminals. We both loathed inside work and internal politics.

We were in our assigned district and on the night shift. It was a warm and muggy night, and area residents were in their front or back yards if they did not have air conditioning, trying to keep cool. We were cruising the neighbourhood, and as we patrolled, we were going through our mental rolodexes, identifying as many people as we could in case something happened in retaliation for the shootings. I saw the suspect whose name had surprised me in front of a house with a group of people. He saw me at the same time, turned, and ran in the open front door of the residence. We called it in and, in hot pursuit, ran into the house after him. You could see the back door from the front door, and he did not run straight through the house. Other police units were arriving and covering the back and sides of the residence. As we checked from room to room, the people who rented the house said nothing. Everyone on the street knew what had gone down with the shooting, and no one wanted anything to do with it. The suspects were on their own.

After we had cleared every room, I was dumbfounded. How could he have gotten away? My partner felt the same, and we decided that the suspect was still in the residence. But where? He was not under the beds. He was not in the attic, nor the cupboards or dressers. It was like he had vanished into thin air. The last room we rechecked was a bedroom. The door swung inward, and for whatever reason, we shut it as we entered. To our surprise, the door on the first search had hidden a small door to a tiny bathroom or water closet. We carefully swung the door open, and there was our suspect, sweating profusely, with a look of resignation on his face. Except for the red gang paraphernalia, he looked just like the remorseful kid I had met years before. No gang to watch over him now. He would get the protection of the gang in prison sometime after he began serving the eight-year sentence he received for his role in the shootings.

Some of the earliest and most violent recruits to the Indian Posse street gang were a group of brothers. They were determined to live up to the reputation for ruthlessness the gang was gaining in Saskatoon. They did not look like much physically and were almost Caucasian in appearance, but they had a cold, pitiless capacity to hurt anyone who stood in their way. Late one afternoon toward the end of my shift, a call came in of a male stabbed at a donut shop close to St Paul's Hospital. The first officer who arrived quickly broadcast the names of the suspects. They were brazen enough to stab someone in front of witnesses even though they were well known in the neighbourhood.

The victim was stabbed for disrespecting the gang members, whatever that meant, and was in serious condition. Although I was fifteen minutes from the end of my shift, I knew the guys would have their hands full, so I left the station and drove back out. I let the officers at scene know I was in the area. I knew the suspects to see them as I had been dealing with them since they were boys. The main suspect, the guy with the knife who did the stabbing, was walking by a parkade when I spotted him. I pulled up in the patrol car and began to get out. He reached behind his back and began to advance on me. I was too close when I first pulled out of the alley, and he had the advantage. I quickly dropped back into the driver's seat and drew my gun. I aimed at his chest and put the car in reverse to create some distance. It was not very dignified as I ran over a small tree, but he was unable to stab me.

Seeing he had lost his advantage, the suspect started to run between some townhouses. I called it in, and units began to pour in for a containment perimeter. I followed him only until I lost sight of him and waited for the K-9 officer to arrive. While I was holding my position, a kid came out of one of the townhouses and told me the suspect had shoved a hunting knife into a planter. I did not want him pointing in case the suspect could see us—the kid still had to live there—so I followed his eyes, saw the knife, and told him to go back inside his house.

The K-9 officer, his dog, and the perimeter officers arrested the suspect shortly after they began their search. The weapon, a hunting knife with a eighteen-centimetre blade, was recovered by the forensic identification officers. It still had fat and blood from the victim on the blade. The suspect, along with his brothers, had been trying to intimidate the victim and other customers in the coffee shop. When the victim told them he was not impressed with their red costumes or bandanas, he was stabbed.

The stabber received a two-year sentence. Oh, Canada! His brothers and he kept committing crimes after his release. Eventually, they were all killed outside of Saskatoon when the stolen van they were driving to North Battleford blew a tire and rolled on the highway.

The Saskatoon Major Crime section did some outstanding work in solving the murder of a witness to another gang killing. She was axed to death and the house she was in set on fire about the time I was transferred from Patrol to the Street Crime unit. By then, I had been dealing with gang members on a regular basis. There was, in my view, no cultural component to them, no honour, no romantic Robin Hoods. Gang members went from individual predatory criminals to pack criminals motivated by greed.

Still, the young gang bangers with all their bravado, gang signs, and posturing, when they were in custody and separated from their gang members, were just scared kids facing an uncertain future as they lay face down, handcuffed, and disarmed. Even high-ranking gang members, when disarmed, in custody, and looking at time, became toothless tigers. Power comes from the pack, and the pack moves on pretty quickly when you are gone.

As long as people keep buying drugs, gangs will continue to flourish. As long as the popular media romanticizes gang life through music, games, and movies, gangs will find young recruits to join them. There are enough kids out there living at or below the poverty line who see the lure of so-called easy money. As long as no one teaches what a true warrior is, there will be Native street gangs.

The police, as is their duty, will deal with you. Be different, and resist for the right reasons.

17

WITH A CLICK

A COUPLE OF YEARS AFTER I was promoted to sergeant, I saw a call in the pending calls queue on the in-car computer to see the complainant at an assisted-living residence who believed he had found child pornography on a computer another resident had asked him to repair. I volunteered for the call as it was a night shift and I did not think this was a two-man call. I did not know a lot about the investigation of child pornography, but I knew possession of it was a crime.

When I arrived at the call, I was met by a young man who explained how the computer came into his possession and who had given it to him. I asked him to show me what he had found. As he turned on the computer I took a ten-second look at the images of children, both male and female, engaged in sexual acts, and was instantly as enraged as I could remember being in a long time. I checked the name of the suspect on CPIC (Canadian Police Information Computer) and found out he was a convicted sex offender on probation. Incensed now, I called for another car so that we could make the arrest without incident.

The beat officers arrived, and after seizing the computer, we went to the suspect's room. He answered the door and then quickly realized why we were there. The suspect was a tall, heavily built man, but he offered no resistance. There is no stereotype physically for sex offenders—he looked like an ordinary guy. I arrested and handcuffed him. Feeling pretty satisfied with myself and with what seemed a straightforward arrest, I transported him to Detention.

I left my report and sent an e-mail to the Internet Child Exploitation (ICE) Unit telling them I had seized the computer. I checked the offence the suspect was on probation for and found he was sentenced to two years in jail followed by probation for having sex with an infant and had only recently been released.

When I returned to work, I was called by the sergeant in charge of the ICE unit. The ICE unit is a newer unit created in response to Internet crime in particular to detect creators, distributors, and possessors of child pornography. It is an integrated unit with members of municipal police forces working with RCMP members. He tactfully explained that I should have called someone from the unit for assistance with the investigation because of the complexity of these types of investigations. He added that if the offender had been the producer of the child pornography contained on his computer, my warrantless seizure may have endangered any subsequent investigations. As the enormity of what he was saying sunk in, I realized that with twenty-four years of experience, I was still learning.

Thankfully, the suspect acknowledged that he had a severe problem and pleaded guilty, landing himself in jail for another year. I learned that in the investigation of some types of crimes, the hurry-up huddle just does not cut it.

The ICE Unit contacted me on a day shift and asked me if I would go with them to check on the welfare of and arrest a male who had failed to appear at court on possession of child pornography charges that morning. I was friends with everyone in the unit and had tremendous respect for the incredibly difficult work they do. The dark side of the Internet means the exploitation of children can be shared with the world in an instant with the stroke of a key. It is complex and challenging work, as well as heartbreaking—you have to be a special kind of person to do it.

In my wildest dreams, I could not have imagined police would be investigating sex crimes that required code-breaking on a military level when I started my career—long drawn-out investigations, and every case involving at least one search warrant. Sadly, there is no shortage of work. The courts try to balance privacy and people's rights with the need to protect children, and in doing so have made warrant applications or affidavits as long as novels. The ultimate goal is catching the creators of child pornography and physically saving children from them. So, the unit works hard to get it right and as free from known legal challenges as possible. Because the crimes rely heavily on technology, the offenders can be very devious to hide their identities so that pedophiles can find each other and share their perversions.

The offenders cover all ages, occupations, and backgrounds, so you cannot even say "He looks like a pedophile" because there is no way to know until they are discovered and charged. So after discovering the suspect, the investigation, search, and seizure of the material relating to the charge, the hardest part of the unit's work begins. The officers have to view each image to see if it is child pornography as defined by the Criminal Code and present it to the courts. I know I could not do this—the rage and anger toward the offender would test my ability to restrain myself. I have only scratched the surface of the unit's mandate and have no intention of speaking to their investigative techniques. They have enough work to do dealing with the pedophiles' countermeasures.

We went to the suspect's address. It was a three-storey house in an older neighbourhood. It seemed huge. The door was answered by a woman identifying herself as the suspect's wife. I let the detective make the introduction and tell her why we were there, but she already knew. Her behaviour was odd, not in a threatening way but definitely not what one would expect from someone with the police at her door. She exchanged a few words with them and let us in. It seemed she could not get out of the house fast enough. My alarm bells started like a ship's klaxon as we began to check the house.

We started to clear the house. It was an older house so it was choppy, and all the rooms seemed to be interconnected. The stairways were narrow and not well laid out. Tactically, it was awkward, with lots of places an armed person could ambush you. We worked our way down to the basement. The stairs to the basement were a nightmare, open to the rear and both sides, but still you had to descend them. I reached the bottom stair and saw a small bathroom to my right and a hallway of sorts to my left. It took a couple of seconds to adjust to the dimness, and then I saw him. The suspect had hung himself from a floor joist. A large swivel screw had been put into the joist, and he had used it to secure the rope he had used to hang himself.

I announced that I had found the suspect. It took a couple of more seconds for the detectives and me to absorb what we were seeing. Once the shock was gone, I went to check his vital signs. He was still warm, but he was dead. I told the detectives that I had it from here, and the patrol constables with me began to secure the scene. At first, it was all business—that is just the reality of police work: secure the scene, call the Identification section to document the investigation, call the coroner, and notify the next of kin.

The man's wife, who had left when we arrived, had apparently gone to the Crown Prosecutor's office to give them the suicide note. Only she knew he was hanging when we entered the house, which explained her bizarre behaviour. Horror can stymie all other senses and cogitative thought. Still, it was hard not to be angry—she let us do a heart-pounding search and left us with our own dose of horror.

When the forensics officer arrived, she began to photograph and document the scene. All the while, the question of who was going to cut him down remained unspoken. He was a thick, stoutly built man, and I could have had the constables do it, but in the end I knew I would do it. The forensic sergeant, after examining the knot, said it was okay to cut him down. I steeled myself because I knew he would still be warm. I was repulsed by the offences he had been charged with, and angry because of what he had put his family and the police through. Ultimately, I was deeply saddened by the desperation and despair of a man so unable to control his base impulses that he saw no other way out than to hang himself. With short, sharp breaths, I held him by the chest as a constable cut the rope. I felt his weight drop, and as gently as possible, I lowered him to the floor, all the while quietly cursing the situation. The coroner finished her investigation, and we waited for the body to be removed to the morgue.

I do not remember a lot more details afterwards except the almost unexplainable actions of the man's wife in insisting the Crown Prosecutor take the note. It was almost as if in her emotional turmoil, she deemed all of us but the prosecutor incapable of understanding her husband's actions and decided he should have to bear the weight of it. I understand denial and how hard it is to accept the unacceptable, and if it were someone I loved I suppose I would have found someone to blame as well.

Internet child pornography is a new level of sexual depravity that enables the pedophile to offend against children every day with the click of a mouse or the touch of a key. Sadly, it is an unforeseen consequence of our switched-on and connected world. Dedicated investigators with iron constitutions do their best to protect our children from them.

Surrounded by new technology, the job still remained about people. *Source:* The StarPhoenix

18

BE YOUR OWN SUCCESS

THERE IS MORE GOODWILL than animosity toward First Nations in Canada, but racism is still alive and well. How we react to it will make all the difference in the end.

I was talking to my youngest son about detectives. He said he might someday want to do criminal investigations. I told him that I was never really interested in being an investigator. I liked the speed and action of patrol work. He corrected me and pointed out that there was a time when I wanted investigate murders. I said yes, but it did not pan out for me.

He said, "Wouldn't you have been the first Aboriginal Major Crime detective in the Saskatoon police force's history?"

I looked at him and said, "Yes, I think so." Then I thought, why I didn't say something like that when I was trying to get into Major Crimes? I dismissed the thought quickly because I knew realistically that that is not the way to get things if you are a First Nations person. As a First Nations person, using your heritage as a wedge to get things takes away from the achievement once you're there. You should stand alone when you compete. It is more honourable and ultimately more satisfying.

I tried out for the Emergency Response team about halfway through my career. My partner had recommended me, and the team had to vote on you before you were given the opportunity to try out back then. I thought that because I was an ex-army guy, I would be a natural fit. It was by far the fairest competition I had taken part in. After two days of rigorous testing, in which I shot paper hostages and did not listen completely to orders, I knew I was not going to be on the team. As well, I learned that although I might be a good leader, I was not a very good follower anymore. I had developed the impatience of a patrolman. If I could not resolve something in a few minutes, I got impatient, and impatience is not a good trait for tactical officers.

In January of 2014, I was speaking to grade twelve English students at a high school in Saskatoon. After about an hour, I began to take questions. Many of the students only knew me from reputation or stories they had heard from other people. One young lady had been intensely staring at me throughout the entire presentation. There is always a chance when doing public speaking as a retired police officer that you may have arrested at least one person in the crowd or one of their relatives. Some people just have a deep-seated hatred for the police, retired or not.

She let a couple of people ask questions before she put up her hand. I pointed to her and told her to go ahead. She then asked, in a very measured and confident tone, "Was your job more important to you than the Stonechild family's grief?" I had not anticipated that question. I repeated her question so everyone could hear.

The answer came quickly, and I explained to her as honestly as I could that you have to pick the hill you are going to die on carefully. If I had pushed harder in 1991, in all likelihood I would have ended up fired from the Saskatoon Police Service for insubordination. As it was, I went on to have a productive career and managed to help a lot of people. I would not have been able to do this if I was not an officer because

I pushed too hard in a system not ready for change. If the exact same scenario had unfolded in year twenty of my career, with the advent of social media, it could have been a different story.

In the end, she was nodding, maybe not to agree, but she was listening. She had waited a long time to ask that question. I thought it was one of the most confrontational and intelligent questions I had been asked while speaking with youths. She made me think on my feet and articulate my reasoning, not just for this case but for many of my decisions over the years.

You have to pick your battles carefully in your work environment. When you are a police officer, you only have a certain amount of control over the battles on the street. Internal battles you do, maybe not in the process, but certainly in the outcome if your integrity stays intact and you trust that the right thing will eventually happen. This is true for anyone, not just the police.

You can choose to feel you are disadvantaged because of your race, or you can choose to see obstacles as challenges. It is, in the end, up to you. If you choose to commit crimes or do drugs, remember it was you who chose it. You can say you were a victim of circumstances, but hundreds in the same circumstance chose not to be victims.

As a Native man, I believe our biggest struggles are behind us. Some of the injustices have been addressed as best as they are ever going to be. I despair sometimes when I hear about problems and I do not hear solutions in the same conversation. I dismiss out of hand people who say that "they" should do something instead of asking what we can do. We as Native people are our own "they." Solutions are in our power to implement with the resources we have on hand. Success breeds success, and the people who find every reason not to help will be the first ones there if we are successful.

Racism has lost a lot of ground in the past ten or so years, especially in the police world. I am not so naïve as to believe it doesn't exist, even among my former coworkers. It is much more subtle, however, and anyone who practises it fears discovery. They will seek to disguise it as work-related or competency issues. I prefer a racist where I can see them.

That being said, sometimes there are work-related or competency issues no matter what your race is. People who cry racism every time there is an incident involving the police weaken the support they would have received when there really is a racist incident. There are far more people who are not racist than those who are. As Native people, we have to be cautious not to create racists by accusing people of racist attitudes who harbour none. When I was a serving police officer and now as a writer, I know the choice of language can make all the difference while trying to establish a point. Calling Canadians who have been in the country for generations colonists or newcomers is as divisive and offensive a provocation as I have heard in a while. I will say it again: I prefer my racist—native, white, or any other race—to be where I can see them.

A few years ago, I took my youngest son to Northern Ontario. We stopped in a small town west of Hearst for breakfast. I saw a restaurant with quite a few cars in the parking lot, which in a small town is usually a good indication of the quality of the food. We went in, and as in all small town restaurants, we seated ourselves. People stopped talking for a moment, then resumed their conversations. The waitress came out with a coffee pot and refilled the customers' cups but did not come to our table. A Native man came in with a thermos—obviously a working man by his clothing—and stood by the cash register. The waitress went into the back and did not come out.

After a ten-minute wait, because I had not encountered this type of blatant racism for years, it dawned on me what was going on. We were not going to be served. The man with the thermos had figured it out a couple minutes before I did and had left empty-handed. I told my son we were leaving. He was confused and hungry. I told him I would explain in the car.

It was my son's first encounter with racism, and it shocked him that this could still go on. The other customers in the restaurant were just as culpable, in my opinion, because they knew we would not be served. The bigger and braver of the people there could have saved us the trouble by telling us we were not welcome.

In 2014, I had just finished a speaking engagement in northern Saskatchewan. My wife and I were headed home and stopped at a gas station with a restaurant in it. I filled the truck and went in to pay. I told the woman working that I was just going to go to the bathroom and I would be right out to square up. She told me that the bathrooms were being renovated and were unavailable. I did not see any sign of construction, and the restaurant was open. I was tired and just wanted to get home, so I paid for my gas and left.

My wife asked why I did not confront the lady. I explained that I did not want to make her a better racist by educating her. A person with racist attitudes will very rarely change those views when confronted. What they will do is get better at being racist, like putting up a sign that the bathrooms are out but telling customers she finds acceptable that the sign is wrong.

I told the story at my next two speaking engagements to emphasise how I felt about racism. If you do not engage with racists, they become like the drunk guy at a party who wants to fight everyone. Left alone, they look, sound, and act stupid until no one pays attention to them anymore. Better to know where you stand with people than be surprised.

We still have a ways to go in Canada. When I told the story in a northern community, people added other locations I should not go to, like this was normal practice. It was sad and frustrating. But while individual racism can be bypassed, institutional racism should always be called out.

At the same time, I have heard some hateful comments come from our own people after they had been arrested. An elderly woman was robbed leaving an evening church service by two young women. When we arrested one for the robbery, she asked, "Why am I being arrested for robbing the white bitch?" Other police officers hear these often racist rants with no hint of remorse. I used to cringe when other officers told me some of the hateful things people would say and wondered how anyone could feel that way.

Racism is out there, and taking the high road is the only way to deal with it. The high road is not entertaining people with racist attitudes or letting yourself be baited into defending your beliefs or self-worth. If you are accused of being racist and you are not, do not give your accuser the time of day. Racism is an emotional issue, and this is why the first thing you do when confronted with it is to check your emotions. It takes the power from them, and unless they physically hurt you, they are nothing.

19

LEARNING TO LEAD

THE MILITARY was where I spent some of my most formative years. Most Canadians remember high school and sports. I had left high school early, so the army became my high school and my transition into being an adult. It was also where some of my strongest leadership lessons came from. The bond of shared experiences in the military is as strong as it is in the police services, in peacetime as well as in war, so a lot of leadership stories I tell are from the army because they ultimately translated into police work and leadership. Some were good, some were bad; all of them, however, were lessons on how to be a leader.

In the military, there are two levels of leadership: commissioned officers and non-commissioned officers. Commissioned officers are people who attend training specifically to learn how to lead and upon graduating training are given a Queen's commission. They start off with the rank of second lieutenant and can rise in rank to the command of the Canadian forces. They are, in essence, the command structure of the military. Usually, commissioned officers were university educated and from families with means. I would not say the social elite, but it's along those lines. Non-commissioned officers (NCOs) are soldiers who start as privates and earned their rank through experience. Non-commissioned officers start as corporals and can rise as high as a command sergeant-major. The difference between the two levels of command is very clear.

NCOs are with the soldiers all the time. They share the same burdens and are beside them through most of their tasks. Officers live separately and are only occasionally with the troops. This is the way things have been in armies for thousands of years.

In the battle school, our platoon commander was a young lieutenant. He was muscular, tall, fit, blue-eyed, and handsome. He looked like an all-star quarterback. He had an air about him, confident and cocky. Our senior NCO could not have been more opposite: Our warrant officer was short and had just the beginnings of a beer belly. His skin was rough and his face hard from years of soldiering. The air about him was confidence based on experience. The other NCOs were three section commanders. Sergeants and master corporals were tough and competent soldiers who worked with quiet confidence.

I didn't know a lot about the platoon commander. He was, for me, almost my complete opposite. It seemed like everything came effortlessly to him. We did not see him all that often but when we did he was always immaculately turned out and never looked tired. I did not even know how old he was, but I guessed around twenty-eight. He was my first real exposure to the concept of executive command. I remember asking myself what made him competent enough to lead us and these NCOs. Was it education and social standing, or was there some sort of leadership training not accessible to the rank-and-file? Tough, experienced, and capable NCOs had to subordinate themselves to the young and cocky lieutenant.

I solved the mystery myself when I realized the lieutenant wanted to be in command and was willing to accept whatever risks came with it. It came down to the fact that the young lieutenant had stepped up and put his name down to be in charge. Like all things, however, command and leadership have a learning curve and sometimes it can be very steep indeed.

When he was around he was in charge, and I never saw him in

conflict with the NCOs, until one day when we were on the range learning how to fire the 60 mm mortars. The 60 mm mortar is basically a metal tube with the trigger on the bottom. It fires mortar bombs straight up in the air, where they arc and then fall down onto the targets and explode. The mortar allows small infantry units to employ indirect fire. The weapon can be operated by one man, but it's more accurate with two. It is truly a weapon you have to get a feel for because it doesn't even have sights. You just angled the barrel until you thought you had found the range of your target and dropped the bomb in. Surprisingly, it was an amazingly accurate weapon. The bomb explodes and its casing shatters into hundreds of pieces of razor-sharp shrapnel. Shrapnel is the leading cause of infantry casualties.

There were small pits on the range for safety purposes and we were in the pits with our NCOs and mortars preparing our bombs and getting last-minute instructions. The lieutenant was not in the pits; instead, he was walking back and forth behind them. We fired our first volley and watched where the bombs landed and got the feel of aiming. The lieutenant walked back and forth over top of the pits telling us the importance of the mortar to small infantry units, especially in defensive positions. We got into a rhythm of firing rounds and switching roles from loader to firer. The lieutenant never took cover, and we were getting close to the end of the firing day.

He told us he wanted to show us how effective the mortars could be in a final protective fire scenario. The final protective fire scenario is when the maximum firepower of a rifle platoon is applied to an area to prevent a rifle platoon being overrun. He explained that we could have more than one bomb in the air before the first one struck the ground and that we could bring the mortar bombs in very close to our positions. So, we started dropping bombs in the tubes and as soon as the bomb left the tubes we would drop another in. We brought the rounds closer and closer to our positions. Still the lieutenant did not take cover. We had bombs exploding forty or fifty metres in front of our positions, exploding while we still had bombs in the air. It was exciting, but all of a sudden we heard the warrant officer yell for us to cease firing.

A piece of shrapnel had struck the lieutenant in the neck. Fortunately for him, the shrapnel was red-hot and cauterized the wound as soon as it hit him. The NCOs immediately went to the lieutenant. The warrant officer was speaking to him in harsh tones. When they noticed we were watching, the warrant officer sent the other NCOs to us and we started cleaning up the firing pits. They kept us busy and distracted. Their faces showed their concern and worry. The lieutenant's attempt to show us how fearless and knowledgeable he was had backfired. He had put the NCOs in a bad position. There had been a major violation of the range safety policies. For the first time, the NCOs needed something from us. They told us we were not to say anything to anybody about what had occurred.

The relationship between the NCOs and the lieutenant changed after that day. It was always professional when he was around, but when he wasn't they would tell us how to do things differently from how the lieutenant had taught us. The lieutenant wore an ascot to hide his wound. After we graduated, I never saw or heard about him again.

Command is easy if you are appointed to it. Having the respect of those you command is a much more fragile thing.

After I graduated from the Princess Patricia's Canadian Light Infantry (PPCLI) battle school in Wainwright, I thought I was pretty hot stuff, a trained albeit inexperienced infantryman. I was ready to serve, ready for any challenges, and ready to take on the world. I was posted to the

Second Battalion PPCLI in Winnipeg. A couple of weeks after I arrived, my warrant officer told me I was to go to the headquarters building to see the company sergeant major. I thought I was in trouble and started rethinking the past couple of weeks. The senior NCOs were the sinew of the infantry and also the disciplinarians.

I very self-consciously went through the doors and up to the sergeant major's office. I came to attention outside his door and reported I was there as ordered.

The sergeant major was a small man. His demeanour and weather-beaten face made him look tougher than anyone I knew. When ordered, I marched in and came to attention. The sergeant major had a file in his hand and did not look up when he ordered me to stand at ease.

Still without making eye contact, he said, "I can see from your file you only have grade eleven."

"Yes sir, but it was good enough to get me here," I replied.

The file went down, and now he made eye contact. He was almost angry, but in a firm, measured way. He told me it was not good enough for him. Unless I wanted to do every crappy job in garrison from that point and until my enlistment ran out in two and a half years, I would have to go back to school. He asked if I understood. "Yes, sir," I replied, and was dismissed.

In retrospect, I am sure the Sergeant Major probably had a laugh about the conversation with the other NCOs and officers in the headquarters after I left. But what was a two-minute conversation for him was a life changer for me. I immediately got my General Education Diploma to get my grade twelve. Later, I took correspondence courses from a college and attended an English course at the University of Manitoba. I never did get a degree, but I learned to keep learning my whole life. I never knew the sergeant major's first name—we would sometimes call him Yoda or the Kraken when he was not around. But he was a leader in the truest sense of the word.

Shortly after I was promoted to master corporal, I was assigned to instruct a course. The Driver Wheeled Course taught people to drive army wheeled vehicles from two-and-a-half-ton trucks to jeeps. I have never been a mechanically inclined guy, but I was assigned to instruct on the cooling systems. I made up a lesson plan, and when the time came to instruct the class I asked the candidates if anyone was a mechanic before they were a soldier. One of the soldiers said he was. I asked him if he thought he could effectively teach the basics of wheeled vehicle cooling systems to the class. He confidently said yes, and I sat down and was taught as much as anyone. I thought I was using my initiative by having a person with knowledge teach the subject properly. Apparently not—the officer monitoring the course failed me on the class evaluation because I did not teach it myself. I have never understood that kind of logic.

The leadership lessons I learned over the years, good and bad, have lasted a lifetime. Still to this day, I loath to eat before everyone else does in a group setting. Leaders should eat after they are sure everyone else has. I would never ask anyone to do something I was not prepared to do myself. I try to set an example in everything I do. When I leave someplace, it should look like I was never there. If something needs to be done, do it, no matter how tedious it may seem, because if it needs to be done someone will have to do it. Service to your community can be as simple as being responsible in everything you do so as not to be a burden on anyone else.

The military is definitely not for everybody, but service to your country and your community is a part of the payback for the quality of life you are privileged to be able to live. For a young person, the question should never be "Why should I?" but rather "Why wouldn't I?"

20

WHAT DO YOU NEED? LEADERSHIP

I JOINED THE CROWD Control team. It was formed shortly after I was hired by the Saskatoon Police Service. The newly formed unit was pretty amateurish at the start. The team was issued 1970s-era riot shields, scratched so badly from improper storage that you could hardly see through them. Cheap motorcycle helmets with visors that had clearly been provided by the lowest bidder were our head protection. We drilled out at CFB Dundurn, a military base just outside of Saskatoon. The team leader positions were assigned to corporals or sergeants merely because they were corporals and sergeants and not because they had any particular skills or training in crowd-control tactics.

I had taken crowd-control training in the military, up to and including mock riots with deployed tear gas. The military training was called "aid to the civil power" and was quite thorough. Because I was so new to the police service, I did not want to point out to the team leaders what I saw as clear mistakes in the training and focus of the team. I thought it would get sorted out after the first time we deployed operationally.

My first opportunity to instruct came along when they asked for a chemical agents instructor. The primary chemical agent back then was tear gas. There were two types—CS and CN—each one having different effects, with the same goal of dispersing a group of rioters. I was familiar with both types, having been on both the receiving and deploying ends. The tear gas we had in stock was the military version from the 1960s and 1970s. The United States used the grenades to clear tunnels in Vietnam as well as for riot control.

For whatever reason, the inspector in charge of the team had an intense dislike for me and would have vetoed my instructing if anyone else had volunteered. In the ego-filled special teams world of policing, we were not considered an elite team, just a team created to fulfill a legal obligation and changing societal expectations. So many organizations, when they create a new team or task force because they have to, often do it halfway. In the early years of Saskatoon's Crowd Control team, this was one of those situations. Just because you give a village a fire truck does not mean that they now have a fire department.

After a year or so and a change in leadership at the top of the department, we started to receive better equipment, protective gloves, actual riot helmets, new shields, and gas masks. We were issued an actual uniform instead of coveralls. We were starting to look and act like a real team. Team leaders were selected for demonstrated ability rather being assigned because of their rank.

In October of 1992, the Toronto Blue Jays baseball team won their first ever World Series. Not being an avid baseball fan, except for a the feeling of national pride at the achievement, the victory was not really on my radar as a significant event, but Saskatoon, unbeknownst to me, had legions of baseball fans, and boisterous celebrations led to a riot on 8th Street, one of the major streets on the east side of Saskatoon. An estimated six to eight hundred overenthusiastic, drunken fans were blocking the street and causing property damage. My platoon was working the night shift, and the regularly assigned patrol members were being overwhelmed.

Our inspector called all the on-duty Crowd Control team members to assemble at the station to get suited up. It sounds impressive, but there were only six team members on duty at the time. The six of us donned our protective gear and fire-retardant uniforms. We grabbed our helmets, riot batons, gas masks, and shields. I was the chemical agents officer, so I filled my vest and pockets with tear gas grenades and a new weapon, plastic ball grenades filled with pepper spray (OC).

We were nervous and excited as we got into a police van, listening to the frantic radio chatter as officers on the street felt they were losing control of the situation. Every policeman's nightmare scenario is losing our ability to protect. We drove to a local 7-11 store's parking lot, and patrol officers, now wearing the old motorcycle helmets for protection, formed on our flanks. God bless them, the fire department had a pumper truck behind us.

In front of us were several hundred drunken people, mostly youths, caught up in the moment, who now had a focal point: us. The atmosphere was intense, loud, and positively electric. It was one of those beautiful and unusually warm October nights, so the temperature and environmental conditions were not going to be our allies as they so often are in the western provinces. After our inspector vainly tried to persuade the crowd to disperse over a public announcement system, we began a cadenced advance, smacking our shields with our batons with each pace.

Like some scene from a medieval movie, beer bottles, rocks, and other objects came raining down on us. Our team leader ordered us to halt to receive the initial barrage, and after it had been deflected, we were ordered to advance once again at the measured pace we had trained for. We received a second barrage, and I could see the smarter and less determined of the rioters begin to waver. The front line of the crowd was so intent on confrontation with the police that they did not notice they were being deserted by the people to the rear. The team leader seized the moment, and we were ordered to charge. It was more of a short dash really, but it got the point across. A couple of people tried to hold their ground, but after being struck with riot batons, they quickly ran or limped away. Patrol officers swooped in and arrested some of the worst and most violent members of the crowd. There were no serious injuries to anyone, and except for picking off a few stragglers who were abandoned by their friends, Saskatoon's first riot in living memory was over. No chemical agents were deployed, and our team had its first successful deployment.

The Crowd Control team was created for this type of situation. It also can be deployed for large out-of-control house parties and search and rescue. All in all, it was not a bad debut. The lessons were evaluated, and we began a new training year with renewed purpose, and within a few months we were looking very much like a professional team.

The same inspector remained in charge, and without explanation I was removed as the chemical agents instructor and replaced by an officer personally chosen by him. I shook that one off and stayed on the team. As long as I did not have to deal with him, the training was valuable.

In 1993, the Toronto Blue Jays were on the verge of winning another World Series. This time, the Saskatoon Police Service was better prepared and an operational plan was put into action to deal with the celebrations. The victory came on my last night off. I could hear the noise of the celebration-turned-riot from my home several kilometres away. Saskatoon's second, much larger riot was in progress. The entire team was called in to work, with exception of me.

The next morning, I drove to work past the scene of the rioting. There was broken glass and property damage everywhere. The guys on my shift who were on the Crowd Control team asked where I had been.

I told them I had not been called. The team leaders told me that they had told the inspector they needed everyone. There had been several thousand rioters and chemical agents had been deployed in quantity to gain the upper hand, and even then it was a near-run thing. The police could have easily lost control or been overwhelmed by numbers, and the rioters could have run rampant.

I had a lot of career ahead of me yet, and I decided that this Inspector was not the rock I wanted to split my canoe on. He was a lesson, nothing more. I resigned from the team shortly afterwards. The inspector took my resignation with a cocky smirk and never said a word. I thought I had shown my money many, many years ago.

Still not done yet, in an interview for a prospective position in the Drug section a couple of years later, he was the senior officer on the panel. He implied that I would not be able to handle alcohol in an undercover role if taking a drink was part of the scenario. I knew as soon as I saw that he was part of the panel that I would not be getting the position, and I did not ask anyone else if he had made the same suggestion.

Pettiness in leadership is soul-destroying for the recipients. So is professional jealousy and ego projection. Sometimes, I wished there was an internal alarm in some leaders that would sound when they were not thinking about how they were treating people. While it was extremely frustrating to be on the receiving end, I used to feel sorry for those types of leaders. So insecure, bullying was the only leadership technique left to them. Still they exist in every workplace, though often they melt down of their own accord. Most of the bullying type of leaders over the years stepped on a career landmine and caused themselves enough damage that they faded from the picture.

In my twenty-sixth year of service, the administration of the Saskatoon Police Service revived an old practice called kit checks. Kit checks meant you had to bring all of your equipment to a senior officer so it could be inspected and checked for serviceability. As well, officers had to account for lost, damaged, or misplaced equipment. In and of itself, it is not a bad practice. The army did them all the time, and believe it or not some police officers were careless with their issued kit. But any practice meant to ensure police officers are properly equipped and ready to serve has to be fair across the board. Applying the rule only to the junior or uniformed officers was demeaning. It is a leadership principle that should never be ignored: apply the rules equally to everyone. To ask officers to present their equipment says on the one hand that your leaders don't trust you to be responsible with what you are issued. On the other hand, it says they care for you and want to see that you are properly equipped. When you're dealing with university-educated and experienced officers, however, inspections carried out without tact and visible fairness are morale-killers.

I was told my kit inspection was coming up. Like so many other officers, I took pride in my appearance and in the serviceability of my equipment. I knew my survival could depend on having everything functioning and serviceable. I have to admit irked me getting my kit inspected in the twenty-sixth year of my career, especially because some of the people doing the inspections had not been on the streets for years. I thought that to the street cops, they would be perceived as lacking credibility. I also knew that I would have to set an example for the other officers and attend the inspection with my usual positive attitude.

The officer who was to conduct the inspection was a newly promoted staff sergeant. We had gone through the Saskatchewan police college together. We had always been assigned opposite shifts, and he had done a stint in plainclothes and had only returned to uniform after getting promoted. At the appointed time, I went lugging all of my equipment to his office. He went through the checklist. We were almost done when he looked at my badge and said I would have to get a new one issued. I was instantly angry and said I would not. I had had the same badge since I started. The badge was battered, dented, and almost all of the gold paint had long since gone. It had been ripped off my shirt in a fight. The patrol car arriving as back up ran it over, and then somebody kicked it into a ditch. It was found by a K-9 officer and his dog afterwards when he did an article search. That badge was me. It reflected twenty-six years of experience. The staff sergeant insisted and said I had to set a good example. All I could think was that I thought I had been setting a good example.

Pride can be dangerous to a career, and I was proud of my badge. I took his requisition for a new badge without a word and left agitated. I procrastinated for about a month and expressed my displeasure to people of equal rank and my supervisor at what I thought was a lack of respect. I know the staff sergeant who had requisitioned the new badge was equally angry that I was not complying. I knew he took it as a direct challenge to his authority as he was trying to establish himself in his new rank. It was going to come to an unhappy and confrontational end somewhere. The staff sergeant I worked for finally told me that this was not the battle you want to go down for. It made sense. I got the new badge. To add injury to insult, I had to buy my old badge back from the quartermaster even though it would have been thrown away if I had not. At the end of the day, it still smarted. Pettiness in leadership is far-reaching and long-lasting to those on the receiving end. Leaders everywhere need to keep that in mind.

In my last years with the Saskatoon Police Service, I found myself acting in the watch commander's role many times. Part of the duties of the watch commander was filling supervisory positions with capable people when a sergeant was on time off or training. With increasing frequency, senior constables were being assigned as acting sergeants more often than in the early part of my career. What level of experience defined senior was changing every year as well—at five or six years you could be considered a senior constable in the years leading up to 2013.

On one of those nights when I was acting as the watch commander, a call came in of a shooting at a downtown hotel. The constable who been assigned as an acting sergeant had about six years' experience, but for a gun call he had few rivals. He was a firearms instructor and a court-qualified firearms expert. I listened on the radio as units began arriving at the scene. Adrenaline in their voices, they calmly called in what was happening, and although my first inclination was to jump in a car and go to the scene, I stayed put. I let the response and investigation unfold. I was learning, albeit a little late in my career, that I did not always have to be there at a scene.

Eventually, it was established that a suspect had entered into the hotel armed with a handgun and attempted to rob the desk clerk. I am not sure if the desk clerk thought the gun was a fake or if he just reacted. He grabbed the gun, and in the ensuing struggle, he was shot through the hand. Staff members and customers came to the rescue of the clerk. The suspect was disarmed and subdued and, in the process, suffered serious injuries requiring hospitalization.

After listening to everything, I phoned the sergeant at the scene and asked what he needed. Once his requests were made and relayed to Communications, I waited until he came into the office to get a full briefing so I could notify the duty officer and local media. Detectives and forensic officers came in to complete the investigative portion of the call.

Months later on a day shift, I was once again acting as the watch commander. I was preparing to turn out the first parade at 6 a.m. to relieve the night shift when a call came in from a local hospital. A prisoner receiving treatment and under guard by correctional officers had used a weapon and escaped.

The two patrol sergeants in the parade room immediately volunteered to leave the station and respond to the call. I thought about it for a second and then told all of the assembled officers to head out without running the parade. The patrol sergeants quickly made a plan for the cordon and search of the hospital grounds. As soon as I heard the escapee was the suspect from the shooting at the hotel a couple of months earlier, I went to the watch commander's office. I did a media release, which included the suspect's photograph. All the while, the radio was transmitting a steady stream of traffic as units were arriving and the sergeants were directing them to their assignments. The hospital and the surrounding area, which included the university, quickly swallowed up manpower, so every member, including plainclothes detectives and uniformed officers arriving early for the seven o'clock shift, were sent out to help.

At 7 a.m., I went up to the parade room to see if there was anyone I had missed, and of course there was. The executive officers were in the parade room. They attended morning turnouts to listen to the bulletins and monitor the proceedings. I dispensed with the formalities and sent out all the constables, uniformed and plainclothes, who were not absolutely committed to something else to try to recapture the suspect, with exception of four officers: two uniformed officers assigned to respond to any emergency calls and two members of the Street Gang unit. The Gang unit members were tasked with the investigation of the escape and all the circumstances surrounding it.

After all of that, it occurred to me that I had not briefed the duty officer prior to assigning the bulk of the available police resources in the city to this manhunt. The duty officer was a newly promoted inspector, and ultimately all the calls I had made were his to make if he had chosen to. I went to his office to begin telling him what I had done and what resources had been committed to the search for the escapee. He looked up and calmly asked, "What do you need?" I was taken aback for a moment and replied, "Nothing. I think we have it covered." He said "Okay. Let me know if you need anything." I walked out beaming from ear to ear. There was no micromanaging, no second guessing, just trust and confidence in the abilities of the officers on the street to get the job done. Leaders leading leaders.

The hospital and university grounds were cleared after an exhaustive search and the area returned to a semblance of normality. The suspect had escaped the hospital and university grounds and was at large. The search now turned to the city itself. Resources were realigned, and unit supervisors took over and assigned tasks. The investigation and hunt continued. By the evening, the suspect was back in custody after a vehicle stop and take-down in the downtown of Saskatoon.

Sometimes as leaders all we can do is give direction and wait for the outcome. The shooting incident and the escape combined show what can be achieved if egos are checked at the door and leaders have confidence in their people's training and professionalism. Strong junior leadership and co-operation between all units in the face of a clear public safety threat without expectation and the need for adulation makes the success of the mission almost a certainty.

There was a constable who was very hard-working and conscientious. He was always immaculately turned out, completed his files on time, and was well liked by his peers. I had been a sergeant for about four years when he started. I didn't realize I could be intimidating to young constables by my reputation. Every time I saw him in the hallway of the police station I would put on my best cranky sergeant face and ask him, "What the !@#$ did you do today?" He would stop and detail every encounter, every ticket and report he left, including what he was going to do. This went on for a couple of months. Finally, I could not stand the guilt anymore and said, "You know I have just been messing with you, don't you?" To my surprise, he said he knew, but my grilling him helped articulate what he did each day. The student teaches the teacher—I loved it.

21

STREET CHECKS

THROUGHOUT MY CAREER, I have had the good fortune of being able to take people out on "ride-alongs" to show them a slice of what police do. Ride-alongs are the practice of taking a member of the community in a patrol car while the officer carries out his or her normal duties. They give people the opportunity to see, hear, and sometimes feel what it is like to be out there every day. Ride-alongs are one of the most effective ways for police services to engage with the community.

Everyone from reporters, prosecutors, politicians, students, and aspiring police officers has sat beside me in the front seat of my patrol car. I always believed it was an honour to be asked to take someone out, but I did not like being told to do so. My measure of what made a ride-along valuable was how open-minded the person was who was coming out with me. The other determining factor was, why did they want to come out? If they came out for a vicarious thrill, they could have stayed home and watched television. If they came out to see how and why police do what they do, they were more than welcome. Except for some experienced reporters who had a specific purpose for coming out with the police, most people when you let them out of the car at the end of the night summed up their experience with, "I had no idea."

Helping people understand the nature of policing was

gratifying, and I learned as much about community expectations as they did about policing. It was interesting to go over stories from when I first started until I left policing and see the maturing of my own insight. At the same time, my values stayed consistent, and if anything became more entrenched. I hoped I always demonstrated empathy and compassion for the people we were serving.

It never ceased to amaze me how people reacted to the physical presence of the police. Uniformed or plainclothes, it did not matter— people almost always changed their behaviour in some way. Surprisingly, the people who were the most comfortable with the police were often those who had been previously arrested by them. If they knew they were not wanted by the police, they would joke and banter with you. Some people, as is their right, wanted nothing to do with the police even if they were not involved in crime. The police had no bearing on their day-to-day life and held no interest for them unless they required their services, like a mechanic's. Most of the different reactions, however, were a result of just not really knowing any police officers or what the police were trying to do.

Some people want to see more of the police, especially in high crime areas, but seeing more of the police sometimes comes with an unforeseen consequence: more police almost always leads to more enforcement in high-crime areas. More enforcement means that people not involved in criminal activity are being checked as if they were, and sometimes people feel they are over-policed.

When I saw people in dark alleys at night, I would always check them and relay to Communications that I was checking suspicious people in an alley. A lot of these checks led to arrests. People were using the lanes to move unseen or to avoid police on patrol because they had warrants or were moving contraband. Not all alley checks led to arrests, however, and I learned to my surprise that a lot of people felt safer in the lanes than on the streets. One group of young people told me that they used the lanes because if they saw gang members they could easily hide in the shadows until what they felt was a danger had passed. I explained my experiences with alleys and we agreed that both views had merit.

I told almost everyone I checked what my goals were: I wanted to make their neighbourhood safer and get the criminals off the streets. Once I knew why they moved as they did, I told them what would make encountering the police less stressful and confrontational. If you are not doing anything wrong and you are checked by the police, be polite and co-operative; tell them why you are in the lanes. Do not run or scatter because a patrol car comes in the alley, even if it seems like a fun thing to do.

Perception plays a huge role on how people see the police. If people only see the police occasionally and never see them smile, nod, or acknowledge anyone, the perception is going to be one of aloofness.

A question I have heard many times when I talk about the area I worked in is "How can people live there?", meaning of course the so-called rougher parts of Saskatoon. The truth of the matter is, people do live there, some by choice, some by economic necessity. So, how do people live there? Day by day is how most of them live. There are working people in these parts of town. There are schools and businesses. There is everything the community needs to grow and flourish. The core neighbourhoods have been changing for the better, year after year. Some of the problems are still there; they are just not as visible as they used to be. Prostitution, gangs, and drug activity still happen on the streets and in some houses every day. There are an estimated 5,000 to 6,000 intravenous drug addicts in Saskatchewan, and the majority are split between Saskatoon, Regina, and Prince

Albert, so Saskatoon has to host its share.

There are still a disproportionate number of families living in poverty concentrated in these neighbourhoods. Poverty can be soul crushing. Unless you have been poor you can never know what it is like. You can become incapable of seeing your way out of your circumstances. Everything can seem like an obstacle. You plan your days by dollars and cents. But although poverty is one of the root causes of some types of crime, it is not by any means the only one: greed, narcissism, and mental illness are in the top tier as well.

Everything in policing is linked in one way or another, and the sooner you learn this inescapable fact as a young police officer, the better police officer you will be. Fines for some offences, like open liquor or public intoxication, seem so counterproductive to helping resolve minor infractions or noncompliance issues. By the same token, this type of behaviour has to be curbed for the community to feel safe and grow. Minor drug possession is in the same category—it still has to be dealt with for the sake of those of us who choose not to take drugs or be drunk in public. So from a street cop's point of view, how do you make it work for everyone? My experience is that you fail your community by not enforcing the law. If a drug addict or alcoholic picks up enough charges, they will eventually change the behaviour so many of us have had to tolerate. Sometimes a stint in jail is what it takes; other times, the person just gets tired of being arrested and grabs one of the many lifelines our society extends on a regular basis.

Minor crime is unfortunately never really minor to the victims. I have heard people say, "Why should I care? It's not my problem." It is a problem for all of us, in higher costs for consumable products as retailers try to recoup costs for stolen goods, in higher insurance costs as companies try to recoup their losses due to claims, and in a higher price tag for administering the law. Minor crime makes us feel ill at ease, and as sympathetic as I am to people in rough circumstances, it still has to be dealt with.

I read an article where the chief of the Toronto Police Service recently suspended the practice of card checks. In Saskatoon they were called a street check card. The reasoning behind the suspension of the checks escaped me. If I lived in a high crime area and the police stopped me and asked what I was up to, I would be pleased that they were doing their job. It would also give you the opportunity to talk to them. Once you get to know someone and know they are not just a head in a car, it makes for a different dynamic. They in turn get to know you. Unless of course, you do not want the police to know you.

I was almost at the end of a night shift on a warm summer night when I saw a man walking barefoot in the downtown of Saskatoon. The man looked like he was in a world of his own. I was not sure if he was high or dangerous so I stopped to talk to him. He was pleasant enough and answered all my questions politely. Still, there was something off about him, so I filled in a street check card and handed it in at the end of shift. One of his unique features was he looked like the classic depiction of Jesus, and not knowing how to word it, that is what I wrote on the card. Years later, some detectives came to me and told me, good job. They explained that the street check card tied the male to several sexual assaults where the victims had used the same term to describe their rapist. The card proved he was in the city at the time of one of the attacks, which detectives then linked to several other unsolved assaults.

In the early nineties, I saw a car parked on 20th Street in Saskatoon with a man in it watching the working girls. There were no businesses open and he did not really have any reason to be there. I stopped behind him and activated the overhead lights. He provided his licence and asked what the problem was. I told him I was checking him because it was good to know who was on the stroll. He did not protest.

He was built like a fire hydrant, and hygiene did not seem to be a very high priority for him. A check on the police computer revealed he had almost completed his parole for manslaughter. He was deadpan and unemotional when I gave him his papers back. I started to fill out a street check card but decided to go a few steps further.

I went back to the station and sent a message to the RCMP detachment where he had been convicted, asking for a summary of the offence. In short order, I received a message outlining the case. The victim had been a nineteen-year-old Native woman. The man had been sentenced to ten years after pleading guilty to manslaughter. It was a very detailed message, so I completed the street check card, filling in John Crawford's name at the top, and attached the message to it.

In the next year and half, John Crawford went on to murder three young Native women and was suspected of murdering two others. Their bodies were discovered in the area of a golf course just outside of Saskatoon. The RCMP quickly identified Crawford as a suspect. I believe the street checks done by the patrol officers on Crawford helped them in the early stages of the investigation and help put an end to Crawford's killing spree.

Late in my career, I stopped a car in the area of St Paul's Hospital to check if the driver had a valid licence. The vehicle was registered to a woman and being operated by a man. Experience has taught me in a lot of cases that the man has the vehicle registered in a woman's name because they have a driving restriction or they are prohibited from driving. Once stopped, the driver was vague on where the woman was. His licence was valid and the car was not reported stolen. His passenger was a well-known criminal, but he did not have any warrants or conditions, so I filled out a street check card in case the car was yet to be reported stolen. Later that night, there was a shooting. The Major Crime detective who was the lead investigator notified me. The vehicle used was the one I had carded, and the suspect along with physical evidence were linked to the vehicle.

The value of street check cards and police recording contacts cannot be understated. To stop the use of them seems so counterproductive. I picked three incidents which came to mind after I read the article. I am sure I could keep going for a while on these. Finding a balance between respecting people's rights and detecting crime will always be a difficult proposition. Police explaining why they do what they do and telling people what their goals are may help.

22

GUNS

DRUGS, GANGS, AND GUNS all go hand in hand. 2015 has been a bad year for gun-related crime in Saskatoon. Our healthy economy unfortunately brings some unsavoury entrepreneurs with it.

A recent call by the chief of the Prince Albert Police Service for carbines for patrol officers started an uproar about the militarization of the police in Saskatchewan. I was asked by CBC to make a comment on one of their news stories about the issue. It felt good to give my opinion on an important issue without having the restrictions I would have had before I retired.

I can see how someone looking from the outside could be concerned about police militarization. From the start of my career until I finished, the physical appearance of my equipment and uniform had changed remarkably. In the end, I was wearing a dark blue uniform with military-style cargo pockets on the pants. My equipment belt was full. My radio was compact, and the extended microphone was attached to a vest on the outside of my shirt. Everything I carried had a proven operational use. But yes, I did look more "military" than when I started.

A carbine, or assault rifle as they were being called in the media, is a military-grade semi-automatic rifle. It is not a machine gun. One round is fired every time you pull the trigger. It requires aiming, and the way it is constructed makes the shooter aim. The shooter is responsible criminally and civilly for each round discharged. The weapon would be military grade because military weapons are by necessity built to last, take the most severe punishment, and work in all conditions. Purchasing patrol carbines would be a thirty-year or more purchase because they last.

The current secondary weapon carried by patrol officers is a pump-action shotgun. While it is a powerful weapon, it is not as accurate, and if forced to use it, the officer is responsible for each pellet. The maximum effective range of a shotgun realistically is forty metres, closer than many areas where an armed suspect might engage the police, such as a mall parking lot or a school hallway. I was always cognizant of the range disadvantage when I went to calls, and I took some crazy chances closing the distance to threat areas when I was a patrol officer. A police officer can effectively engage an armed suspect with a rifle at one hundred metres or more.

When I first started with the police, we carried a .38-calibre revolver. Coming out of the military, I was immediately contemptuous of this inadequate, underpowered weapon. I doubted its range and ability to stop an armed offender. You had to open the wheel where the bullets went to unload it, and then, even with speed loaders, had to load and close the weapon to get back into the fight.

Our use-of-force options in Patrol were limited to unarmed combat, striking with a wooden baton, or the .38-calibre revolver and the 12-gauge shotgun. We wore heavy leather boots and equipment belts. We were supposed to wear ties and the police cap on patrol. We were limited to the front pockets of our pants and police shirts to carry what we needed outside of our patrol cars. Some officers wore bullet-proof vests and some did not.

The modernization of police equipment started in the early 1990s. The public did not want to see police fist-fighting or hitting people with wooden batons, or failing that, shooting people but not stopping them if they needed to be stopped. Officers on the street wanted better equipment to be able to do their jobs safely. We were issued new pistols, a semi-automatic, magazine-fed, robust, modern weapon. Police shootings did not increase, but my confidence in my ability to defend citizens and myself did.

OC spray was issued as a low-risk, intermediate use-of-force option. OC is a pepper-based irritant spray that is sprayed into the eyes of a resisting suspect. It is painful and it forces the eyes shut. Commonly referred to as pepper spray, it reduced the need to physically fight with resisting suspects and lowered the possibility of injuries to both suspects and arresting officers resulting from those fights.

Even something as simple as the colour of the uniform shirt was found to make a difference to how people perceived the police. Studies found people trusted and respected officers in dark blue shirts more than the light blue we were wearing. Eventually dark blue shirts and pants with cargo pockets were issued. The tie was discarded for a mock turtleneck. Nylon duty belts, lighter and more secure, replaced the old leather belts, greatly reducing back problems for officers. We were allowed to purchase our boots and we were free to choose lighter and more modern types of boots than had been issued previously.

In the early part of my career, body armour or bullet-proof vests were worn under your shirt. They could be hot and uncomfortable during our twelve-hour shifts. Vests can now be worn externally so officers can remove them when they are in the station leaving reports or to air out after incidents where they had to run or fight.

Our portable radios became smaller and more effective. Some of the stories I have told illustrated how inadequate radio equipment affected my ability to respond to some situations. The extended microphones and longer battery life have enhanced officer safety.

Weapons and driver training improved as standards and public expectations rose. The training and equipment the police have acquired in the years prior to the recent spike in gun violence in Saskatoon will now stand them in good stead as they attempt to get it under control. Increased public scrutiny and awareness of police procedures with the advent of social media made our police service and police services across Canada modernize, but modernization is markedly different from militarization.

I have read many interviews with people who have attacked or murdered police officers. The common factor in their decision to attack was the officer's appearance. If the officer looked unprofessional, unprepared, or sloppy, this factored into the attacker's mindset. A fit, well-trained and -equipped, and confident officer can look intimidating to the public, but those same police officers should inspire confidence in the people they protect. My personal experience was that the ability to do my job over the years was improved by hard-gained experience, and the modernized equipment I used did not militarize me or the way I policed.

Since I left policing, I have done a lot of public speaking. High school students have asked me some of the most challenging questions. You will always get questions like have you ever shot someone? Have you ever been shot? My answer is thankfully no to both questions. But then I expand on the answers.

Guns and police have always held a fascination for people, probably because in Canada, law enforcement personnel are the only ones who carry weapons in full view of the public. It sometimes shocks people when I tell them that if I had been forced into a situation where I had to shoot someone in my policing career, I would have. It is one of things that as a police officer you had best have sorted out in your head before you are involved in an incident where your or someone else's life depends on your willingness to act.

I have always taken shooting for granted. I grew up around guns. They never scared me. I knew you had to be respectful of their destructive power and handle them properly, but they were, in the end, only tools. I have fired thousands and thousands of rounds as a civilian, a soldier, and a policeman. Thankfully, I have never had to shoot anyone. I have been very close to firing, but the suspects gave up in the nick of time.

In my career with policing, I dealt with thousands of people in all sorts of situations. So have my former co-workers. In the average year in Saskatoon, about ten thousand people get arrested. Over the span of my career, there were a quarter of a million arrests. Each arrest entailed taking someone physically into custody. During this period, there were four police-involved shootings by Saskatoon police. I knew or had worked with all of the officers involved at one time or another. I know all of them to be good people and dedicated police officers. I also know shooting someone affected them all.

Anyone who says Canadian cops are trigger happy really has no idea of the enormity of a police-involved shooting. The common denominator of the shooting where Saskatoon officers were involved was that the officers were fighting for their lives. The personal toll is huge. Police, like firefighters and paramedics, are hardwired to save lives. Shooting someone is contrary to everything first responders do. No one I knew was ever the same afterwards.

Replica firearms look so real now that, in the heat of the moment, it is virtually impossible to tell the difference between a pellet or replica pistol and a real one. At night or in low light conditions, it is even more difficult. I have heard dispatchers broadcast that the complainant in gun calls suspected the gun was fake. I would get on the radio and tell the officers responding not to assume anything and not to let their guard down.

After a shooting, people often ask why the police didn't shoot the suspect in the leg or arm. This is like trying to throw a rock at a swaying branch after running. If you are under stress and in the fight-or-flight mode, your body rushes the blood to your core. Your accuracy and motor skills are affected. You might get lucky and hit the branch, but more than likely you won't. Police are trained to aim for the biggest part of the target to ensure they stop the threat: the centre of mass—the chest.

One observation I have made over the years is that people with no prior experience with firearms often shine in police firearms training. They have no preconceived notions about firearms, for the most part, so they learn quickly and properly taught weapons-handling skills stick with them long after they graduate. Believe or not, I used to hear some officers complain about having to go to firearms training. I was not one of them. Shooting is a diminishing skill for most people. If you do not practise, it will show very quickly. Very few people are instinct shooters.

Qualifying with your firearm is a job requirement, and you will be pulled from the street if you cannot do it. The pressure on police officers to qualify every year looms like tax day. Some officers stress themselves so much that they will fail on the first try and have to re-qualify. Qualification standards have been moving consistently higher, and the training has been keeping step. Training hard for something you hope you never have to do is just one more thing that has to be done. It has to be done with dedication and purpose throughout your whole career.

On a Sunday day shift in August 2006, a call came in of a shooting at a house in the west end of Saskatoon. A twelve-year-old boy had been shot with a sawed-off shotgun and was badly injured. Several units responded along with firefighters and paramedics, all of us arriving at about the same time. The boy was on the stairs to the second floor, looking very pale. A comforter had been placed over the wound to staunch the blood flow, and paramedics quickly got him out and to the hospital. Everyone in the house was traumatized and afraid. I had never met the family or the victim before. The house appeared clean and normal, like the house of so many young families everywhere.

The parents had no idea there was a shotgun in the house, much less a loaded sawed-off shotgun. One of the constables at the scene was becoming the platoon firearms expert, so I had him recover the weapon and make it safe. As the supervisor, I contacted Major Crime detectives and the Forensic Identification unit to attend. Witnesses were separated, and I stayed on scene until the night shift sergeant took over. You never really walk away from a call like this, and the next day I went down to the detectives to get the story and see if there was anything else I could do.

The story emerged that the boys had bought the shotgun from a male who lived a couple of blocks away, and they were passing it around upstairs when it went off. They only knew his street name, which was unique, and as soon as the lead investigator told it to me, I knew who it was from a traffic stop and ticket I had written months earlier. When I wrote the ticket, the man had dropped the name of an officer he knew. I went to the officer and asked if he knew the guy. He told me he did and said that was what they used to call him years ago. The nickname became the street name he used. A check of his address revealed that he had left town after the shooting. A helpful neighbour told me he was up north, and with the help of the RCMP, he was arrested and brought back to Saskatoon.

In spite of how illegal guns are portrayed in video games, the reality is not nearly as exciting young people think. The boy who was shot would live with a lifelong disability.

A pre-street ritual; everything needs to be checked including every round in the shotgun. *Source:* The StarPhoenix

23

THE OTHER OFFICERS

I AM GRATIFIED TO HEAR that the stories I have told about my experiences during my service with the Saskatoon Police Service have given people a new and different perspective of the police. I must say, though, I never intended to do any disservice to all the other police officers who were not in uniform patrol. The reality is that there were many different aspects of policing I never experienced, and my perspective is limited to the streets. I really only touched on the most visible parts of police work. The other stuff is no less important to the victims and investigators.

I did have some interesting glimpses into these other areas, like Commercial Crime or Fraud. At one point, a group of fraud artists hit on a particularly vulnerable group of persons to make them accomplices in a scheme to defraud a major bank. The suspects would go to the bars in the Barry and Albany hotels and look for women who needed money. They would approach them for their bank cards and personal identification numbers. They would make empty-envelope deposits in these women's accounts over a three-day weekend, and then the women would report their banking card stolen on Monday or Tuesday. The surveillance video would show a hooded male making the deposits, thus exonerating the women, or so the women thought. What the fraudsters forgot to tell them was that the cardholder was responsible for the personal identification number and was on the hook for the funds. The criminals quickly moved on to other women. In most cases, the women had no money to cover the empty-envelope deposits and the bank was out the money. It quickly ran up into the tens of thousands of dollars. These were very satisfying guys to arrest. The women I just felt bad for.

Another scam was selling false advertising for phone book covers in hotel rooms. One particular fraud artist literally did it all across Canada, moving from province to province when the scam was discovered and knowing that any issued warrants would not be extended outside of the issuing province because the amount of the individual frauds was low, usually under five thousand dollars. I actually stumbled onto this guy by accident. Another officer had taken the fraud report. I was not aware that a report had been taken—it had not been entered on the system when I took the report for the second time. The complainant, already a bit embarrassed that he had been defrauded, was very abrupt and rude with me as there was already a language barrier. I did get enough information to identify the suspect and went to his last known address. I arrested him as he was leaving and a seized a briefcase full of evidence. He had warrants outstanding in Saskatchewan issued by the RCMP for similar offences.

Feeling pretty good about myself but not knowing a lot about the fraud laws and how to investigate further, I went to the Fraud office to get some help. The detective told me that they were all busy with their own cases and as this was relatively minor on the fraud scale, I was on my own. I sorted it out as best I could, and this suspect ended up going to jail. He had, however, successfully defrauded people out of thousands and thousands of dollars across Canada before it all caught up to him in Saskatoon. His victims were all small-business people.

The scale and scope of fraud and white-collar crime requires a special kind of police officer, and I was not one of them. Business frauds, bank frauds, seniors' frauds, and counterfeiting all require patient and thorough investigations by dedicated and educated officers. The losses can be in the millions. I was not up to those types of investigations.

I took a surveillance course when I was in the Street Crime unit. There is a unit where patience is a virtue. As a result, I never worked there. There had been a series of violent sexual assaults, and the detectives had identified a suspect. We were tasked to keep surveillance on him at the start of a day shift. The suspect was at his workplace and we were to keep an eye on him until the arrest warrant was signed. I thought it would be an easy hour or two and we would be able to take him into custody. The day dragged by, in spite of my impatient prodding and telephone calls. The team leader said we had not been given the go-ahead. The workday ended and the suspect left his work, and now the static surveillance turned mobile, which is a lot more challenging.

My partner and I kept calling the team leader, who in fact did not really have any say over when this suspect could be arrested, giving him updates and stressing him out with our impatience. The suspect, though unaware, had a chance of losing us in the downtown traffic, and having a suspected rapist in the area was not sitting well with us. As we crossed a bridge into the Nutana neighbourhood of Saskatoon, we finally got the word to take him. We stopped his car and ordered him out at gunpoint. We were in plainclothes and the takedown took place directly opposite a popular ice cream place on a warm summer day. As we were handcuffing the suspect, I could see the customers watching us and probably wondering what their city was coming to.

The long hours of static surveillance and then the high-intensity mobile surveillance coupled with the takedown put the brakes on my surveillance aspirations. I realized I did not like not being in control of the tempo and outcome of investigations. I could not just walk away either because surveillance is part of working in a plainclothes section. The next surveillance task was a static one. A vehicle was set up outside a house targeted for a search warrant to keep an eye on who was coming and going. The rest of the unit was close by. To my own surprise, I volunteered to go in the static vehicle. It was a sickeningly hot day. I knew there was a clear end to the period of surveillance, so I hunkered down and called in any people or vehicles coming and going. Over the radio, I could hear the Emergency Response team deploying. I got up to the window to warn of any last-minute movements when the team deployed flash-bang grenades. No one warned me, and all I saw was white flashes for about five minutes. Flash-bangs are a concussion-only grenade which explodes loudly and emits a bright white light. If you do not shield your eyes, you are temporarily incapacitated. After the all-clear and in-custody signals were given, I got out of the surveillance vehicle and swore off surveillance for the rest of my days, although I really enjoy that aspect of hunting.

Over the course of my career, I have called on the services of the Forensic Identification section countless times. We called them I-dent for short. Like all officers at some point, I thought that my cases were the most important and just expected that they would take first priority. Forensic officers are probably the most extensively trained of the speciality sections. Every piece of evidence worth recording is captured on film. Every sample, no matter how small, is documented and seized. Every death and injury of significance is attended to. In Saskatoon, this means twenty or so Forensic Identification officers deal with all the forensic evidence generated by four hundred-plus police officers in a city with one of Canada's highest crime rates year after year. I do not know how they keep up. Once again, not my thing—there was too much meticulous attention and too many details for me.

Detectives who investigate break-and-enters to homes and businesses are another group who get things done quietly. As a patrolman, a call to a "break-and-enter over with" meant the home- or business-owner had discovered the crime after it was over. Most people feel deeply offended and affected when their homes are entered and their possessions stolen or destroyed. As a patrol officer, you looked for evidence, called I-dent if there was any evidence, left your report, and moved on. If you were able to, you tried to make the victim feel secure again and hoped they could move on. Then the case was assigned to the detectives in the Break-and-Enter section.

When a call came in of a break-and-enter in progress, it was exhilarating. Your body would pump adrenaline because you knew you would have the chance to catch the offenders in the act rather than taking reports with little or no hope of satisfaction to the complainants. K-9 officers would be on the air and on the way in seconds. These calls were almost always thrillers. At one call, I saw an open window at the side of a house. Officers went to the front and back doors to cut off an escape, and I crept along the wall to get under the window in case the suspect used it. I was rewarded seconds later when two hands grasped the windowsill and a head appeared. Pumped up and not thinking, I grabbed the suspect by the collar, surprising him and yanking him out the window. As he landed, I realized he was a big guy. Luckily, the surprise and landing took the wind out him and I got him handcuffed.

At another break-in in progress at night, my partner and I quietly rolled up on the house. We found the point of entry. Using hand signals to indicate which way we were going to move, we entered the residence and could hear the suspect upstairs. The suspect, hearing sirens, came running down the stairs and was double-clotheslined by my partner and me. The suspect was in his early forties and a notorious break-and-enter suspect. His arrest was very satisfying.

People who break into homes and businesses come from all age groups and criminal backgrounds, and it is not only young people who do these robberies. Some rings are very organized and able to move the stolen property in many different ways. There are some break-ins where a suspect just sees an opportunity and acts impulsively. Most break-and-enter offences are for a purpose—obtaining property to sell in order to buy drugs, or stealing tools or machines for resale to less-legitimate business people—and a lot is organized crime-related.

The detectives do not get to do the clotheslining or collaring. They piece each case together painstakingly, looking for patterns, using informants and Crime Stoppers tips to build cases. They execute search warrants and get confessions. This is how it gets done.

Now to Traffic. Nothing makes people more aware of the strengths or weakness of a police service than traffic enforcement. Traffic-section members are in uniform except for special projects. Traffic enforcement affects everyone, no matter how law-abiding you are in criminal matters. Taking the cell phone call when you are on the way to daycare to pick up the kids might initiate the only contact you ever have with the police in your whole life. I have found that once you were identified as a police officer at a social outing—and so many police officers will be able to relate to this—the conversation would be about tickets. The unfair ticket Uncle Joe got. The unfeeling ticket issued to the cousin on his way to a funeral. People get emotional when it came to traffic enforcement the way I wish they would about the more serious issues. Traffic-section officers probably get the most abuse of any police officers on a daily basis. If you want verbal abuse as a police officer, just stop a law-abiding citizen under stress for a traffic violation.

I did not help with the team effort. I was never a big ticket-writer. It was a constant source of irritation for my supervisors when I was a constable. I would write tickets for unregistered or uninsured vehicles, not having a licence, and moving violations that caused accidents. Other than those, most often a lecture was the worst you would get from me until the last few years of my career when the crime rates started to drop and I had more time to do traffic enforcement. As the economy of the province improved, the number of vehicles on the roads increased along with the number of moving violations.

Early in my career on a bright spring day, a young man driving a sports car at a high rate of speed westbound into the glaring sun passed a car on the right that had stopped for two elderly pedestrians crossing in a marked crosswalk. The sports car hit them, seriously injuring both. The driver was unrepentant, and it seemed to me an obvious case of dangerous driving causing bodily harm. I left a detailed report and charged him. I received a note from the administration complimenting me on the quality of the report. Months later, I received a notice from the Crown Prosecutor's office that the case was not going ahead. There was no explanation for why it was not proceeding, just a note specifying that the time period for issuing a ticket had expired. The young man received no sanction whatsoever short of what penalty the government insurance company imposed financially.

A couple of months later, I saw a vehicle driving at approximately ninety kilometres per hour in a fifty-kilometre zone by a shopping mall in the late evening. When I stopped the car, it was the same young man from the accident. He had the cocky look and smirk he'd had the first time I had dealt with him. I could not help myself, and I said to him, "You're not going to be satisfied until you kill someone, are you?" I wrote him a ticket for driving with undue care and attention. When the matter came to trial, my comment was raised by the defendant. The traffic magistrate asked if I had said this. I confirmed that I had, and he was convicted. I did learn that when you issue a ticket, never make comments or give lectures. Do one or the other, never both.

These cases early in my career demonstrated to me the need for technical expertise in accident investigation and full-time traffic enforcement because the stakes can be quite high. Accident investigation and reconstruction has become increasingly sophisticated with computer technology both in-car and in the re-creation of accident sequences. Long gone are the days where a measuring tape and a few pictures would do in criminal, civil, or traffic court trials. The officers who do these have to have a mathematical and analytic mindset my grade-nine math mind cannot even begin to comprehend.

Traffic officers are passionate about public and vehicle safety. They bear the brunt of the ill will directed at the police by the non-criminal element of the public, until we need them to slow speeders in our neighbourhoods. Some people will try to get away with anything they can when it comes to vehicles, insurance, and driver's licences to save money. They pose a hazard for the rest of us using the road. Traffic officers set up vehicle inspection check-stops because poorly maintained vehicles are dangerous. Bald tires, poor brakes, rusted frames, and exhaust leaking into the passenger compartments of vehicles are just some of the hazards they uncover. It doesn't matter what part of town they set up in, wealthy or poor, for some people keeping their vehicles maintained is just not a priority. If the Traffic section did not take unsafe vehicles off the road, they would be criticized, especially if a vehicle's condition caused a fatality.

Patrol is a big part of policing, but it is not the only police perspective there is to tell. Policing has many different areas where officers can go besides uniform patrol. Passion and dedication will always remain the benchmarks of a job well done in policing, whether it is spending a year or more on a missing or murdered person's case, or months reconstructing an accident or crime scene. The people with an eye for detail are as necessary as the officer willing to kick in the door at an assault in progress.

The sun has almost set and now it really begins. *Source:* The StarPhoenix

24

HIGH

WHEN I THINK OF THE STRUGGLES we as Canadians have with drugs, I often wonder what Winston Churchill would have said if he were in charge of Canada's drug strategy. Would he have said, "Let us remove ourselves from this struggle because it is too hard"? "Swing open the gates and let them in because resisting this destruction of our youth is futile"? I am pretty sure he would not.

In 2013, every murder in Saskatoon was drug- and gang-related. Even the tragic murder of a mother in her home was a case of mistaken identity related to a drug debt and gang hit. Tragically, the killers gunned down the wrong person at the wrong address. It made her murder all the more senseless and horrifying. If not for the appetites of drug users, Saskatoon would have had the lowest murder rate in recent memory. In my opinion, any movement to legitimatize illicit drug use as a valid personal choice or social condition dishonours the innocents killed to allow the trade to flourish. I have heard all the arguments for new approaches, and based on my experiences as a police officer, the present system is a gate best left closed. It is really all about what kind of country you want to live in. I would venture to say that the majority of us don't want to be involved in a wide-open social drug experiment. I don't.

When I first started with the Saskatoon Police Service, the learning curve on drugs was a steep one. In short order, I learned that just about anything that could be used to get high, was used. Intravenous drugs like Talwin and Ritalin were in high demand, and the addictions to them were debilitating. Talwin is an opiate painkiller. Ritalin is a drug used to stimulate the central nervous system. Together, they were referred to on the streets as T's and R's. People I arrested called it "poor man's cocaine." Prescription morphine was gold; it had many street names, like down, greys, and mo. The pill trade was something I had never heard of, and getting a look at this dark side of drug abuse was an eye-opener.

Cocaine was not common, at least in the area I worked, because it was so expensive. Pharmaceuticals were obtained in as many ways as you can think of, from high-risk drug store robberies all the way to trolling cancer patients in hospitals. The demand was relentless, so drug dealers, who were often addicts themselves, were very imaginative. The risk of a used syringe poking you during searches became and remains a real concern to police.

Marijuana, hash, and LSD were still around and well represented on the streets. Magic mushrooms came and went in cycles. The bars and the malls were the hotspots for low-level drug trafficking, the kind that uniformed patrol officers like me in the late eighties and early nineties dealt with on a regular basis. Bars like those in the Barry and Albany hotels were like the operating storefronts for the drug dealers, and there were not a lot of law-abiding citizens who went there every day. Everyone knew or at least had an idea of what was going on there. In my opinion, the Midtown Plaza at that time in Saskatoon was a different story.

The Midtown is exactly that: the largest shopping mall in Saskatoon, right in the heart of the city. It was a place where criminal activity seemingly took place in view of everyone, and visible crime is what erodes the public's perception of their community. Mall security were learning as they went, but they were not peace officers, and their mandate was limited as to what they could legally do.

When I was still new to Saskatoon, I met a friend for coffee at the mall. There were no Native police officers my age in Saskatoon at the time, so in spite of my short hair, a man came up to me and asked if I wanted to buy some weed at five bucks a joint. I told him no and, as this was in the pre-cell phone era, watched as he walked away.

A week later, I was in the mall again, and the same man came up and asked me if I wanted weed a second time. This time, I arrested him. There were not really any guidelines in place at the Saskatoon Police Service for what you were supposed to do in a situation like this. He had about twenty kilograms of weight on me, so the arrest could have gone bad very quickly. I think his shock that I was a cop was what saved me. With the help of mall security, I held onto him until the officers who were working showed up. He had nine joints and a lengthy record, so he received a nine-month sentence. We crossed paths many times over the rest of my career. He went from drug dealing to fraud, theft, and break-and-enters. I think he was wearing out, though, because in the last couple of years he dropped off the radar.

What he did do was cement how I felt about drug dealing and criminal activity in the mall, especially in the food court where the dealers and stealers congregated. I volunteered to walk the beat shortly afterwards. Most police officers who have walked the beat will tell you it was their favourite assignment. The interaction with people is the biggest reward. Walking the beat for me meant twelve-hour shifts walking in the downtown and Riversdale neighbourhood. When you walk everywhere, you quickly learn where the trouble spots are and who occupies them. I took it as an affront that people shopping had to move around these people and tolerate their activities.

The mall security staff was on board as I began to learn how to police in a city, with the mall being one of my biggest challenges. There were some very good security officers who dispelled the mall cop image very quickly. They knew who was who and who did what. Working together, we managed to arrest dozens of people on warrants for drug offences and weapons possession. Word was getting out, and people began to get up and leave in groups if I came into the food court.

As much as I was learning, the criminals were learning, too. Junior people held the drugs and took the fall for possession. On one trip through the mall, I saw a young offender who had a warrant outstanding for a minor offence. I knew the chances were good he would have drugs on him, so I went to arrest him. He reacted just as I thought he would, pulling away and trying to escape. What I was not expecting was the butt of pistol protruding from his lower back. I took him down hard and people in the mall began yelling at me that he was just a kid. Once I had the handcuffs on him, I pulled out a Colt .45-calibre replica pistol from his waistband and stuck it in my duty belt. People stopped yelling and quickly walked away. He went on to being a pimp first and then a prolific drug trafficker and high-ranking member in a street gang. He was still in jail when I retired.

In the same time period, an informant tipped me to a man selling LSD tabs in the food court. His instincts kicked in when I started in his direction and he ran. After a foot chase, I caught him in the bathroom area before he could flush them away. Each tab of the nine he had left was marked with an identifying mark of a Chinese dragon. Another informant had told me who was supplying the Chinese dragon LSD, and he was still in the food court. After another officer came and took custody of the first guy, I went back into the food court. The alleged supplier saw me coming and stuck something in his mouth, landing me in a legal limbo. I could not grab him by the throat to stop him from swallowing whatever he had put it in there, but if it was multiple tabs of LSD, he could be in trouble medically depending on the quality of the dose and the quantity. For people not familiar with LSD, it is a hallucinogen with a high that can last anywhere from eight to forty-eight hours. It comes in a liquid, which can be poured on sugar cubes or dabbed on colourful slips of paper. His smirk and confidence began to fade as I did not do anything, just stood there. Eventually, he swallowed what was in his mouth, and not knowing what I could do, I walked away. Nowadays, to err on the side of caution, I would have detained him and called for an ambulance. We were all still learning, and although as much as I disliked what he did, I worried about him afterwards. I did not see him for several months. He eventually resurfaced, kept on dealing drugs, and moved on to armed robberies. He was in and out of jail for the rest of my career.

I learned the majority of shoplifting arrests were in fact drug-related, as addicts shoplifted or boosted goods that could be traded in the bars and hotels for drugs. Some were bold enough to take orders for specific goods. But as much as I was learning, I had the feeling that I was missing just as much. Someone had to be calling the shots. None of the drugs just appeared on their own. I felt there was always a bigger picture, although some low-level dealers' operations might have been just that, hand to mouth with no real structure. Low-level drug dealers and semi-organized shoplifters were labour-intensive visible criminal elements who made people feel unsafe. I rationalized that it was police work that had to be done by someone, and I enjoyed it, so I stuck with it until I was eventually bumped off the beat back into a patrol car. I was not actually bumped—it was more of a request from my co-workers who wanted a chance to get out on foot as well.

Like shooting, sports, or hunting, you get better with practice, and I became better at spotting low-level drug transactions. My fiancée, now my wife, was working in a downtown restaurant and I was living in an apartment right behind the police station. She was almost done work and I started to walk over to pick her up. As I was passing by another restaurant just a block from the police station, I saw two men in a car with a big block of hashish between them. It looked to be at least a kilo. I walked by without staring as they got out and went into the lounge of the restaurant. My heart was pounding as I ran to the corner and waited for a police car so I could wave them down without the suspects seeing me and still keep their vehicle in sight.

There is never a cop around when you want one. After a couple of minutes, I gave up and ran to the station and grabbed two constables. In my excitement, I had forgotten to write down the plate number of the car, so when we got back I was relieved to see that it was still there. The two men were in the lounge when I approached them. One was a big guy, obviously a biker from the clothing and Harley Davidson motorcycle accessories, and he protested. The other guy was smaller and looked like a university student. He just started sweating.

I arrested them both and located a few grams of hashish on the big guy and a brick of 481 grams on the smaller man.

We were all fairly new guys so, satisfied with what we had, the arrests were taken into the station. I walked over. Because the big guy only had a small amount and there was no compelling reason to hold him in custody, he was released on an appearance notice. Knowing what I know now, he probably ran back to his car and got the hell out of Dodge with the money from his sale and the rest of the brick of hashish I had seen.

I went and found a Drug section detective. He explained

how we were going to get a search warrant on the residence of the man with the large quantity in his possession. He explained how hashish was cooked in bricks and how the location of the break in the brick I had proved it was broken from a bigger piece. We did the search and came up empty. I had the buyer not the seller, but I was learning. Several hours later, I finally met my girl like I was supposed to. How I got her to marry me I will never know.

I had been passed over for the Drug section, which was just as well because so many people by then knew me to see me. The guys who were successful were a whole new breed. They were more than willing to try new techniques, and they came in just as the drug scene in Saskatoon was exploding with cocaine and an improving economy. Saskatoon moved to an integrated Drug section pairing with RCMP members.

Street gangs were evolving as well, and drug houses began cropping up in different neighbourhoods. This presented new challenges for uniformed patrol officers because everyone in the neighbourhood knew what was going on, and it appeared to them that the police were unable to check the brazen activities. Because the Drug section only had so many members to allot to each threat or investigation, patrol officers had to find their own way of making a visible difference.

The "broken window policy," in which police enforce all laws and deal with minor violations with the same vigour as major offences has come under attack recently in protests in the United States of police shootings. It has been said this practice unfairly targets minorities, and as a matter of fact it does. Criminals are in the minority, and they do get targeted. It doesn't seem to be much of an argument. As a former street cop I can say it is the quickest way of dealing with drug houses and high-visibility crime.

Active criminals can be an arrogant lot. They will walk in front of vehicles, cross against Don't Walk lights, and then sneer or swear at people going about their lives. They can have thousands of dollars of drug money in their pocket and they will still shoplift. They just can't seem to help themselves. So, enforcing minor laws leads to weapons and drug seizures and immediately useful real-time intelligence that helps solve more serious crimes, up to murders.

It is overzealousness on the part of less experienced officers where police run into problems. There are no shortcuts when it comes to formulating grounds to check someone on the street when you're a cop. The pairing of junior and senior officers together is in most cases good practice. Senior officers have had more experience articulating why they stopped and checked someone. In many cases they have been tested in the courts during trials and know what is acceptable.

25

COCAINE AND METH

I GOT MY FIRST COCAINE ARREST in the early nineties. Cocaine had been coming down in price, so it was inevitable that it was coming north. I saw a guy in the Albany Hotel who had an outstanding warrant, and he tried to run out the back door when he saw me. As I was grabbing him, he dropped a small packet of white powder. Up until then, intravenously injected prescription drugs had been the most destructive addiction out on the streets. Cocaine brought a whole new dimension to the misery. The idea of purposely loading a syringe with cocaine of an unknown quality and injecting it into my veins scares me to death.

The arrival of cocaine in quantity in Saskatoon changed the drug scene into a free-for-all. There was so much money to be had. Everyone wanted a piece of the action. The street gangs quickly set up houses and carved out their territories. I had to relearn how to do drug arrests. Cocaine is easy to dispose of, making speed and surprise necessary to get the evidence needed to convict. We all needed to learn.

I arrested a woman on outstanding warrants and seized two syringes with a white powder in them up to the 15cc mark. When I questioned her, she candidly told me that they were called dry packs and that was how small quantities of powder cocaine were being sold on the street. A couple of shifts later, my partner and I burst in on a gang member as he was loading cocaine into needles. He was arrested for possession for the purpose of trafficking in cocaine. He was not our intended target—we were there searching for someone else—but his arrest confirmed the woman's information.

Pre-loaded syringes have become very common over the past ten years with the introduction of seemingly limitless free needles. In Saskatchewan, as part of the harm-reduction strategy to reduce the incidence of HIV-AIDS and hepatitis spread by using dirty or used needles, millions of free needles are distributed every year. Quality spoons, alcohol swabs, and rubber tie-offs are part of the giveaway as well. I read a 2008 report on the needle program released by the Saskatchewan government. The report writers interviewed many people, including police chiefs, but nowhere in the report did I see an interview of a street cop. The sad fact of any well-intended program is there are always some people willing to take advantage of it, just sometimes not the people it was intended to help. The study went on to say that the needle distribution did not show an increase in the number of IV drug users, but unless they all moved into my district at the same time and it coincided with the program, I think it did. I felt the number of IV drug users increased with the availability of needles. People who were otherwise scared of HIV-AIDS and were thus deterred now tried IV drugs because the dealers told them they could do it safely. Cocaine arrests became common for patrol officers in my area, and the amounts seized went from a couple of dry packs or rocks to ounces. Substantial amounts of cash were being seized as well.

Addicts never bought in bulk in case they got ripped off for their stashes. As a result, the foot and vehicle traffic to the drug houses was staggering—with needled cocaine, an addict shot up on average several times a day and, if they were on a binge, up to twenty times a day.

Some dealers let the addicts shoot up before leaving; others sold through holes in locked doors. We would be arresting someone in a lane behind a drug house and people just went to the front door instead. They were so brazen and so addicted.

They were twenty-four-hour operations, and every time I did not have a call, I rolled into the areas where these houses were located. In the past, these were usually rental properties on poorly lit streets with easy access from overgrown alleys. Now, with the massive amount of cash that drug sales generate, unfortunately drug houses can be anywhere. The Drug section only had so many resources and a whole city to police, so we made do. The troops made some good arrests, and these all helped with the intelligence picture when the drug investigators needed information to build grounds for search warrants.

It was a little Wild West for crime for a while, and then methamphetamine threw its toxic hat in the ring. At first, it seemed it was only the white men and women using it on the East Side and in the North End. Just as ecstasy was a young person's alternative drug, the people in my area seemed to be avoiding meth, or gibe as it was called on the street at the time. Methamphetamine users are like human roman candles: use, get addicted, and the physical deterioration was remarkably rapid. People can be addicted to pills and cocaine for years without a marked decline in their appearance. Meth showed no such mercy. The addicts would not sleep for days on end. They smelled like cat urine or body odour. Their internal wiring was so frazzled that their movements were jerky and spastic.

During my time with the Street Crime unit and later as a Patrol sergeant, I had the privilege of working with a couple of officers who displayed an outstanding understanding of the meth scene and the people involved in it. Meth is a cooked drug made from readily available ingredients in home labs. Meth addicts will dumpster-dive to get credit card receipts and use stolen cell phones to order items to sell. SIM cards from cell phones were hot commodities. The amount of energy and effort these addicts put into supporting their habits was daunting.

One of these officers received information that one of our notorious female meth dealers had sent two of her guys over to a hotel to collect a debt. Two constables and I went there and intercepted them coming down some stairs armed with improvised clubs. We seized their cell phones, and when the dealer texted one of them, the officer who had received the information texted back to see if he could get her to come to the location. A couple of text exchanges later, the dealer wrote: "If this is you ___ [the officer's name], better luck next time." Impact. He was getting under her skin. I loved it.

I was more of a spectator or backup officer as these officers systematically took down one dealer after another. On a day shift, we arrested a man on an outstanding warrant and there was a text message on his phone. The message warned the man that the officer I was with was in the area, but two minutes too late.

I would often tell people who worked for me when I was a sergeant that anyone can drive around and take reports. Tackle problems head on and you will make a difference. Drug enforcement— as challenging as any policing issue—made them better police officers. Many of them went on into other units like the Drug section and the Gang unit.

One of the downsides of a booming economy is that more money means more drugs. The drug trade spread over the entire city. No area of Saskatoon seemed to avoid having a home used as a base for dealing by gangs. The Drug unit was seizing larger and larger quantities, into the multi-kilo weights. Guns were being seized more often with the drugs. The Emergency Response team was being used to execute high-risk search warrants.

The drug trade and the addictions it creates keeps going every day in Saskatoon and the rest of Canada. Still, the day-to-day business of the police goes on: traffic accidents, school visits, break-and-enters, and all the other things police do daily. We can never throw our hands up because the quality of our community is at stake.

For of all the hand-wringing and analysis of this problem, it still comes down to personal choice. The choice to use. The choice to sell or traffic. The choice to break the law. Thankfully, there are people who choose to protect us from the people who have made those choices, and people who choose to help them when they choose to stop.

As I finished this chapter, another young person died from an accidental overdose from counterfeit OxyContin, the third to die in Saskatoon in a period of five months from counterfeit pharmaceuticals. The number of cocaine and other drug overdoses was not included or reported in the news stories I read.

26

COURTS, MARK YOUR ARCS

IN THE ARMY, when you settled into a position or stopped for an extended halt, the officers, when assigning positions, would show you your left and right arc of fire or responsibility. The principle was, each position would be mutually supporting, as all of the arcs would be overlapping. Unless you were on the far flanks, someone was depending on you, and you on them.

Society can learn from this basic military principle. Whenever I hear someone in any organization oppose a new idea with the standard, "We've always done it this way," I shudder unless they qualify it with a firm, demonstrable, "because this way works." Because the stakes were so high in military matters, bad ideas were quickly discarded, or died with originator. Necessity made for simplification.

In December of 2014, I was asked to speak at a Court of Queen's Bench justices' conference. I was honoured and intimidated at the same time. As I was preparing for the event, it became clear to me, as a former police officer and now a citizen, how I felt about the courts. Through all the chaos, societal changes, and new technologies during my career, the most consistent institution has been the courts. Every detected crime and arrest eventually ends up in a courtroom, where after argument there is a finding made by a judge, or judge and jury, guided by the law. Someone, and I do not remember who, told me years ago that when you are in a hurry, slow down—it is the best way to avoid mistakes. The courts at all levels slow down the pace of the action and reaction. The formality of the courts is their very strength.

I do not know how many criminal defence lawyers there are in Saskatchewan, each one of them anxiously planning and researching the defence of accused persons, as is their duty and obligation. What I do know is that they outnumber the prosecutors by the hundreds. The Crown—the prosecutors—are an elite group of lawyers beholden to the law and the Crown to seek justice for all of us. Sounds dramatic, but however dramatic it sounds, it is the basic truth. They do not work for the police. In fact, the most serious dressing-downs I got as a police officer were from Crown prosecutors because they wanted to get it—justice—right.

When I first was promoted in the army and later with the police, I was a bit shy and awkward when people would address me by rank. At first uncomfortable, I thought it over and came to the conclusion that they were respecting the rank. The respect for the position had been earned a hundred or a thousand times over by the people who had held the rank before me. So when someone called me sergeant, I would never diminish the respect by telling them to call me Ernie.

All the justices, judges, and lawyers involved in the system have carried forward the respect earned by the officers of the court before them. Nothing should be allowed to take away from the formality of the courts. To call a justice or judge your honour, or a lawyer sir or madam, is one of the few signs of respect still required and expected in our society. The respect sets the stage and makes everyone slow down to intelligently arrive at a solution or verdict in an increasingly complicated world.

In my career as a police officer, the most vile and serious criminals were the ones who believed that the system had no power and that there would never be any meaningful consequence to their crimes. Discharges, fines they would never have to pay, and extended probations all served to empower criminals, regardless of race. I have heard criminals upon being arrested who are utterly disrespectful to the court process. They would say things like: "I don't give a shit what the judge has to say, I'll be out the next day." "I could do five years standing on my head." "I'll just get probation. "Give me all the fines you want, I won't be paying them," and some much more explicit turns of phrase. Only on rare occasions did they ever repeat them in the prisoner's dock. As a policeman, I too have said things and heard other officers say things outside of the court that I know we would never have said in court. Criticizing rulings or judgements we did not agree with was natural given the limited view we sometimes had of the whole proceedings.

There are some decisions made by the courts—such as the recent Gladue decision in Edmonton—that were clearly outrageous to the average person. Like stories about police misconduct, they will get an amazing amount of attention—especially now on social media—that the day-to-day administration of justice doesn't attract. However, the courts have been the most consistent institution in Canada for years. We cannot let the respect diminish. In my opinion, the courts have been the champions of First Nations in the past twenty years. Let us not squander the opportunities these decisions have presented.

The average person will not have a lot of contact with the criminal courts. When they do, though, it is almost always unintended and often unwanted. Unless they are summoned for jury duty, either they were a victim of a crime or a witness to one. If any of these occur, the obligation on them is to be forthright and honest in their testimony to help the process that maintains the order in our society.

The police gather the evidence and present it to the Crown.

The obligation of the police is to be honest and unbiased in gathering all the evidence. Police officers leaving their reports have to be aware that the reports they are leaving will be read by many people, possibly for years afterward, so reports to Crown prosecutors have to be clear and concise.

The Crown analysis of the case decides if the case will move forward through the courts. Clearly defined areas of responsibly and mutual support help this process along. It is the job of the police, Crown prosecutors, and the courts to educate anyone who has come into this process and help them through it every time something happens, no matter how many times it has to be repeated. Justice well explained and well thought out, including telling it like it is, requires this.

Assaults and sexual exploitation of people with intellectual disabilities is one of the most challenging and disturbing crimes to investigate. Making arrests in these cases challenges the self-discipline of all police officers.

One summer day in 2006, shortly after I was promoted to sergeant, a call came in from a woman who alleged she was being beaten and confined by her uncle in a notorious apartment block along 20th Street. I knew the location and from the apartment number, who the uncle would possibly be. An older, solidly built man with a demonstrated propensity for violence, he was, I believed, more than capable of inflicting pain.

I met two constables at the location, and we stormed up the stairs to find out what was going on. At the door of the apartment, we could hear what sounded like a woman crying inside of the apartment. We announced ourselves, and I turned the doorknob. The door gave way an inch or two, but it was barricaded with a refrigerator. The male constable was a big man, and together we put our shoulders into the door to force it open. The suspect tried to brace the refrigerator with his back and gave me just enough of a target with his head that I was able to punch him in the face. The punch was enough of a distraction that we managed to push the refrigerator almost on top of him and gain entry.

The female constable went straight to the victim and immediately upon seeing her injuries called for an ambulance. The suspect was quickly overpowered and placed into handcuffs. Slightly bloodied, he was still defiant and full of hate. When you actually catch someone in the middle of a violent attack and stop it, you see a person at their closest to being an animal. With guttural noises and glazed eyes, they make you fear for the weaker people they prey on.

In this case, the victim was a tiny woman, not even five feet tall and weighing all of eighty pounds. She was bleeding, and her body was blackened by bruising. I recognized her from previous encounters. She was a sweet lady in her late twenties. She had limited cognitive ability and operated with the innocence of a twelve year old. Because she was of age, she was able to buy and consume alcohol, which made her all the more vulnerable to being victimized. She always called me uncle. To see her so injured was enough to enrage anyone.

The suspect was a big man, weighing over two hundred pounds and standing six feet tall. Built like a farmer, he was thickly muscled for a man of his age, and his hands were like steel. In any other situation, he would look like a grandfather, but in the hot, dirty confines of the two-bedroom apartment with a bloody victim lying on a bed just feet away, he was definitely not anything like that.

The victim said, "Uncle hurt me, uncle." As if I were playing the Angry Cop in an almost television-like moment, I told the constable to get the suspect out of my sight. The victim was transported to the hospital and the suspect was jailed. The courts and the Crown Prosecutor's office managed to get the victim into an assisted living home outside of Saskatoon. The Crown prosecutor assigned to the case contacted me and advised that given the suspect's long and violent criminal record, they would be seeking a designation of long-term offender if he were convicted. I was elated. This man was a predator, and older or not, he would not stop preying on people.

When the time came for trial, there was an issue surrounding getting the victim from her new home to court. I volunteered to drive there and bring her to court on my own time if there was a problem because I felt so strongly that she deserved some justice. The offer was officially discouraged. I think the line of thought was that it would give the appearance of coaching the witness and would be an impropriety for the defence to exploit at trial.

As it turned out, at trial the victim was unable to convince the judge beyond a reasonable doubt that she had been assaulted by the suspect. The victim was able to say that she had been beaten. She was unable to articulate what else I suspected had occurred. In spite of the evidence, there were only the two of them in the apartment with the door barricaded when the police arrived. The defence was able to create a reasonable doubt in the mind of the court. The suspect-now-defendant sat in the court with his shirt done up to the top button, repeatedly asking for people to speak up because he was hard of hearing. He looked every bit the senior citizen wrongly accused and confused by the proceedings. Long past was the bloodlust and fury in his face on the day we arrested him. The cunning of the predator can never be underestimated.

The victim left the group home after he was acquitted, and I dealt with her a few times at the bars before I left policing. The suspect avoided me as much as he could and was arrested for another assault on a woman in the last months before I left. I do not know the outcome.

There are many stories like this. Sometimes in spite of all the best intentions of a lot of good people and organizations, there will continue to be some people who slip through and away. Just knowing it can and does happen helps us caulk the places they slip through.

Marking your arcs happened every time we stopped moving in the army because the reasons why it was done never changed. The courts are not perfect. But they slow things down enough to let us look at the whole picture and take some of the emotion out of our reactions. The courts, in my opinion, are the last bastion of order in our increasing complex country. Respect for the courts, which we expect so much from, should never be allowed to diminished.

27

VOIDS

IN 1996, A MURDER OCCURRED on my days off. The murder took place in the centre of my district. When I came to work, I found out the victim was a guy I had arrested a couple years earlier. He had apparently been beaten at a house where he had been drinking with several other people. Blooded and injured, he had gone to his brother's apartment building. An ambulance was called, and the victim was taken to St Paul's Hospital, where he died. When I heard the names of the people involved, I knew them all. I had been dealing with them almost continuously over the years. One of the men I immediately suspected was more than capable of committing a murder. He was one of those guys who ingratiated themselves with a hard-core drinking crowd and violently took whatever he wanted from them. He was younger and stronger than the rest, and he was always a threat.

I went to the detectives and told them what I knew about this guy. To my surprise, they told me he was a co-operating witness. He had written a letter to them and said that he was terrified of a male who was at the house when the beating occurred and accused him of the murder. I knew the male he was accusing. He was a big guy, but more often than not he was one getting beaten up. My alarm bells were going off, but it wasn't my case, and I was a Patrol officer. With uncharacteristic speed, the detectives arrested and charged the male being accused by the co-operating witness on the strength of his and his girlfriend's statements.

The story came out that this group of people had been drinking Pink Panthers—hairspray—late at night and into the early morning hours at the house where the victim received his beating. These guys drank hairspray because it was up to 90 per cent ethanol alcohol. The most popular brand came in a pink plastic bottle. In a drunken stupor, the suspect was supposed to have taken a heavy metal bar and beaten the victim because he had drunk the last bottle. The co-operating witness told investigators that he had fought with the suspect and took the bar away from him. Another male took the bar outside and put it in a City of Saskatoon garbage bin. In a stroke of bad luck for the investigators, the garbage was picked up and in the landfill before the police were even aware this incident had occurred.

Months later, I got a call from the investigators asking if I could help track down the witnesses and serve them subpoenas. I had been anticipating this and had been keeping track of everyone. I found the co-operating witness's girlfriend in a local bar. The detectives had asked me to serve her a subpoena and bring her down to the station for a further interview. When I brought her to the car, she told me that everything she had told detectives was a lie. She told me that the co-operating witness, her ex-boyfriend, had beaten her and told her what to say to the investigators, and had beaten and threatened everybody who had been at the house. She said that the story he told was true, except that he was the one who had wielded the metal bar, and the person awaiting trial was the one who took it away from him. I made my notes and brought her to the detectives. I told them what she had told me and left an investigation report.

The preliminary hearing for the accused went ahead shortly

afterwards, and she did not answer to her subpoena. A warrant was issued for her arrest for failing to attend court is a witness. I found her a couple months later and arrested her. She told me she had missed court because her son was very sick in another province and she had gone there to be with him. She repeated the same story about her ex-boyfriend and his culpability for the murder. She did not waver in her details. I transported her into cells and contacted the investigators.

Shortly afterwards, the charges against the accused man were stayed, and he was released. It didn't take him long to get back with the drinking crowd, except now he was a bit of a local celebrity with his friends. The man I had thought was responsible for the murder stayed in my area, and I arrested him several times. Every time I arrested him, I told him that I knew what he was and that his time would come. His hatred for me grew and grew until he threatened to kill me in front of my partner after we had arrested him for a rape. He received a jail sentence for the threats and disappeared from town shortly after he was released.

I never heard anything from the investigators. All the people who were present when the victim was beaten began to die. The man who was arrested and charged was murdered a couple of years later, stabbed to death at a house in the Pleasant Hill neighbourhood of Saskatoon. The girlfriend of the man who made the initial accusations against him died from health problems associated with chronic alcohol abuse. Another man who had been at the house suffered the same fate shortly afterwards. The man who had allegedly taken the metal bar and put it in the garbage can drank himself into a barely functional state and has since died as well. Now there was only one person left who could tell the story in court, other than the person I suspected was responsible for the murder in the first place.

Over the next few years, the Major Crime section was totally revamped. New investigators, new techniques, and new leadership made it more professional and more accountable. This case continued to gnaw at me. The victim's family was not affluent, nor could they ever be privy to all the details of the investigation of the murder of their family member. I don't even know how many of the victim's immediate family were still alive. Still, his death was not avenged and no justice had ever been served. Sadly, almost everyone who could have righted this wrong was dead. Still, at the time there was still a living witness. The cold-case guys had just finished with the case of a murdered missing mother, which had taken a lot of their time and efforts. I met them at a restaurant and asked if they would give this case a second look now that they were free. I should qualify this: cold-case homicide investigators are never truly free; there are up to twenty cold cases still being investigated in the city of Saskatoon at any given time.

What a quantum change had taken place in the Major Crime section over the years! The cold-case investigators sat and listened. There was none of the arrogance and visible disdain I had got so many times before when I tried to assist an investigation. I was not made to feel like I was an interloper or a busybody. I felt we were all part of a team, with the same goals.

There's been a lot of attention paid to cold cases in recent years. Television has dedicated several series, both fiction and nonfiction, to the subject. The reality of cold cases is they are paper and boxes. Some physical evidence is stored, but for the most part they are boxes of papers and memories. The violence, passion, and urgency have long since passed, and only the need for closure remains. The Investigators re-examined the file and found a sworn statement from the ex-girlfriend of the man I suspected was responsible for the killing in the first place. In the statement, she clearly implicated him and the steps he took to point responsibility elsewhere. The statement had been misfiled with another homicide.

The investigators asked if I could locate the two witnesses. They were located and interviewed. One of them was a male who had thrown the metal bar in the garbage. I had arrested him many times since the murder. He was a well-known drunk and had even been featured in a front-page story in the local paper. People and even some police saw him as a character. I did not. For years, every time I arrested him, I talked to him about this murder and how it was time for him to man up and tell what had happened. I would put him in an interview room with a picture of the deceased on interview room table and leave the room. Every time I came back, the picture was turned over, and he would yell and swear he was going to kill me. He was interviewed by the investigators, and the consensus was that his years of chronic alcohol abuse had made him incapable of being a witness. He too died shortly afterwards.

The other witness, a woman, provided collaboration for the ex-girlfriend's version of the events. It looked like the investigation was going to get some new life, but events have a way of slowing things down, and a DNA hit on another file had the investigators going in another direction. The DNA databank found a match to an unknown suspect from a brutal murder and rape of an elderly woman from the 1980s. It was horrific case. The arrest and conviction of the man responsible gave all of us who were around at the time a sense of grim satisfaction and long-overdue justice.

One of the investigators retired shortly afterward, and I thought this case had gone cold once again, but the remaining investigator kept working on it. He called me and told me the case had gone over to the Crown prosecutors for an opinion. The whole case would rest on a confession by the accused. The woman he had interviewed had also recently died. So there it sits: final justice for the victim precariously perched on the investigators' ability to obtain a confession to a crime sixteen years ago to which there are no longer any living witnesses.

As my career was wrapping up in 2013, the determined investigator gave me one last briefing. He retired shortly afterwards, one of the best and fairest investigators I had ever known. The suspect was interviewed. Years of alcohol abuse made him incapable of confessing— his recollections were so badly befuddled that the suspect himself could not be sure if he did it. So there it was, an unavenged murder with every person involved dead before the suspect could ever be charged.

In the police reporting system for concluding files, there was a category you could check off that I rarely ever used as a police officer: "Beyond the control of police." I was not the concluding officer, but this was the one time I thought this could not be truer. It was a void.

A tremendous amount of planning and work went into getting to this unsatisfying conclusion. What I do know is that at least we tried. My admiration for the investigators and the Crown for their efforts fill me with pride. There are some very noble and honourable people I have the privilege of working with, whatever the outcome.

I wrestled with writing this story, but in the end there were many lessons to be learned from this case for police officers. The big one is to always keep an open mind when investigating any crime. Murders are the extreme example of this. The first person to put their hands up as a witness can sometimes be the suspect. Everyone has value, and if you remember this in everything you do, cases like this will not slip away to the point that this one did. Policing is a serious business with high stakes on the outcome you are charged to provide. Only a few people would ever benefit from these lessons if this story sat untold.

28

ALWAYS A CHANCE

A COUPLE OF YEARS AFTER we were married, my wife and I stopped to pay a bill at a downtown business. We had small children, so even bill paying could be a production: car seats, diaper bags, meticulous planning, and whatever it took to get it done. I paid the bill, and the woman taking the payment asked, "You don't remember me, do you?" Until she spoke, I had not. Hearing her voice, I knew right away who she was: a woman from a violent domestic situation, battered in an assault committed by her husband a couple of years earlier.

At first, I felt a bit awkward. I always tried to keep work and my family as far from each other as possible. The woman then told me that she had listened to what I told her that night. She got out, and her kids were happier now. The call came back to me as she spoke. This woman at the time was a stay-at-home mom, raising the children while her husband worked. Her self-esteem was tied to the success of her marriage and children, and because of this, she endured physical violence from a man frustrated with his life. When he had a bad day, she had a worse one. He demeaned and insulted her in front of the kids, and when he drank he would hit her. The woman in front of me was a world away from the woman I met the night I went to her house. She appeared confident and relaxed.

I remembered the night I was at her house and the amount

of convincing it took to get her to provide a witness statement so we could arrest her husband. I understood the fears and doubts women had in making the decision to make a statement in a domestic assault case. I would always try to explain the process and what I had seen from experience happens afterwards.

This type of incident or something similar occurs every day in Canada. Stopping it and making offenders accountable was grim and rewarding police work. I would tell every woman who would listen that it was not her fault, no matter what she was alleged to have done by the abuser. A man has a choice to walk away when angry. He makes the choice to hit. In my experience, if a man hits a woman and she does nothing, he will do it again. The seriousness of the injuries almost always increases as a victim's self-esteem slips away. I would explain how if their children see abuse, they will have a higher chance of being an abuser or being the victim of one. A lot of this you would think is common knowledge nowadays, but I think having a police officer sit at your kitchen table and lay it out for you makes a difference. I would give the women as many alternatives as I could and hope for the best.

Domestic violence knows no barriers in social status, income, or education. It thrives if the victim or witnesses are silent. These are also sometimes the most difficult of cases to prosecute. The dynamics of love, shared parenthood, and income all wreak an emotional toll on the victim.

A call came in from a relative of some children who had fled their apartment in winter and ran barefoot ten blocks through the snow to get help for their mother, who was being beaten. When we arrived at the apartment, we found the mother in the kitchen, bleeding and injured. The woman's husband was in a bedroom, covered in his wife's blood, his fury spent. I was close to a very dark place when my partner told me he was not worth it. I handcuffed and arrested him. He never said a word. My partner probably saved my career. She was right—he was not worth it. It is not the job of the police to reap revenge on men who hit women, as tempting as it may be to do so at some calls. In all likelihood, it just reinforces the abuser's belief that using violence is the best way of expressing himself.

Most men who abuse women do not fight the police when they are arrested. The ones who do are the most hateful and violent of the lot because they believe they have every right to beat their families and the police have no right to interfere. I have no idea how many times I have heard men say things like "The bitch won't show for court" or "She will let me come back tomorrow—you're wasting all of our time." They count on the fear that their violence has brought to the victim. I have also heard women say things like "They made me write a statement" and "I love you" as the husband is being led away in handcuffs. I have had women tell me, as they were being loaded on stretchers, "You have ruined my life" by arresting the attacker. All street cops can relate stories like these from domestic calls.

Injuries at domestic calls can go all the way from bruises to murder. Even though police officers can go to thousands of domestic calls every year, often involving the same couples over and over again, they need to treat each one as seriously as the next. They need to provide as much knowledge as possible to the victims. Some people listen, some get out, and even though you may never see them again, they will remember you. Persistence works when working with victims. Never stop trying to help them out of the situation they are in. It does not always work, but when it does, it will make all those times you wanted to throw your hands in the air in frustration worth it.

There is something about criminals that draws certain people to them, in particular younger women. Maybe it is the devil-may-care attitude or their lack of inhibition. Either way, I have seen many women gravitate toward them, and even after they had been assaulted or forced into criminal activity, they remained fiercely loyal. I never quite understood it. Still, the pattern repeated itself over and over. Most of these relationships ended badly when the women were discarded after they were of no more use to the criminals. Race, education, or profession made no difference in the choices they made to be with criminals. Corrections officers, lawyers, and social workers all fell under the spell of criminals during my career, and it ultimately ruined theirs. Yet there were a few women who, in spite of all the obstacles, some self-inflicted, broke free. Those stories are, for me, all the more special.

I met a Métis man from northern Saskatchewan a couple of years into my career who could have been anything he wanted. He unfortunately chose to be a criminal. Solidly built and good looking, he was intelligent and articulate. He struck me as a natural leader. He was addicted to IV drugs and committed armed robberies to support his habit. The robberies were often committed with firearms. He had been in the criminal scene a few years before I started with Saskatoon police. In short order, our paths began to cross on a regular basis.

His girlfriend or common-law wife was Métis as well. She could have adorned the cover of any magazine. She was as intelligent, if not more intelligent, than he was. Every time we checked them on the street or had reason to deal with him, she would study us. She appeared to be making mental notes of the police positioning, listening carefully to the radio and the particular police language we used during the contact.

In one incident, I was aware that he had an outstanding warrant for robbery. At the beginning of a night shift, my partner and I were having coffee at a restaurant at the corner of Avenue U and 22nd Street West, and he walked by the window. We saw each other at the same time, and he immediately began to run. A foot chase ensued, and we arrested him. He was about fifty–fifty for convictions on his armed robberies, and for the one the warrant was issued for, he was sent to prison.

While he was inside, she turned to prostitution to get by. Every time I talked to her, I would tell her she was better than that and to get out while he was incarcerated. She would listen without comment, smile, and nod.

A couple of years later, he was out and she was with him again. She had probably never left him and maintained a prison relationship. Prison made him bigger, stronger, and meaner. He went right back to drugs and robberies. I was working a day shift and knew a warrant had been issued for him, charging yet another armed robbery. I was right in the centre of the Riversdale neighbourhood of Saskatoon when I saw him. I jumped out of my patrol car to grab him, but he slapped my hands away and ran again. I was by myself as it was a day shift. I chased him right into a house. He did not know the people inside. He kicked down the door and went into the house in an effort to escape. The occupants, a single mother and her children, were terrified. Thankfully, he surrendered in the house, and besides shooting hate daggers with his eyes, he did not resist being arrested. He went back to the penitentiary, and she went back to the streets. She disappeared before he got out of prison.

Years later, I got a call from Communications staff saying that she had called and asked for my cell phone number. I told them it was all right to give it to her as it was my work cell. Shortly afterward, I got a call from her. She told me she had met a nice guy, was married, and had children. I was beaming. She called to thank me for believing in her. I was so happy. I could see her smile and felt I had done something for someone just by being persistent. In a job with so many sad and tragic endings, it was a high point. It was an "I made a difference" moment, even if it took years to accomplish. I hope she is still happy. She will know who she is if she reads this.

In a profession like policing, those "I made a difference" moments can get missed in the day-to-day work. You may never know how you affected someone or how they affected you until years after the encounter. The time to reflect is a luxury not afforded very often if you're a street cop. I have the time now, and every story I have written leads to yet another story. I think I am not quite done yet.

"The Riders lost?" Night shifts made you miss a lot. *Source:* The StarPhoenix

29

SLIGHTLY DENTED BUT GOOD TO GO

I HAVE NEVER BEEN OFFICIALLY DIAGNOSED with post-traumatic stress disorder. During my first medical in years at age forty, I told the doctor that I was struggling with anxiety and he told me rather curtly that that was not his department. I never pursued it any further and did not go to a doctor for years afterward. I did not fully realize the physical and psychological effects of my service until I left it for good. When you are doing your duty day after day, everything just seems like episodes in a drama. Sometimes you are shocked, but mostly you just take chaos in stride.

The huge infusions of adrenaline seemed normal, and I admit were part of the draw of the job. Lights and sirens, high speeds, and foot chases can become addictive. Arresting wanted suspects for serious crimes and overcoming violent resistance are tests you take on a regular basis. You embrace it and become hypervigilant. The trick, in my opinion, is for serving officers to find the balance between action and well-being using the experiences and lessons of the officers before them.

Now more than a year out of policing, I have a little more perspective and insight. There is honour and obligation in what you do, but some of the psychological scars were self-inflicted—I could have left Patrol and done something less stressful. It was the arrogant part of me that believed that no one else could do the same job as I did, or that the people in the areas where I worked would not be as well policed if I just left them. The truth of it is, they will be well served by the next generation as long as they are of the same calibre as those I was taking for granted when I left.

I thought I had been open about the effects the job had on me in my first book, but my wife Christine encouraged me to be more open afterward. My wife was with me during pursuits, arriving at homicides, foot chases, and fights; not literally, but during the nights when I relived these events in troubled sleep. I flung around so much that she called her sleep "defensive sleeping." It started in 1999 after a pursuit where the fleeing driver killed a married couple on Valentine's Day. My wife told me I was reliving the pursuit in detail and going through the motions of driving and repeating what I had said that night. I scoffed and told her she was exaggerating. Then she told me details I had never told anyone else. I also used to stomp my foot on the floor in my sleep. I would notify next of kin and describe crime scenes, sometimes just fragments of an incident but sometimes in detail. On reflection, Christine and my family must have had some eerie nights.

The reality is, opening up about post-traumatic stress is stressful. Acknowledging is healing, however, and though I acknowledge the toll begrudgingly, I am about 70 per cent all right with what I have seen and been part of.

Trauma imprints, but some memories just keep lingering. It is memories of people in pain, where you were relegated to the role of a witness or a participant by circumstance, where you felt the most helpless—no handcuffs or arrest, no resolution, and to be truthful, no way to train for these type of calls attended to nearly every day by first responders all across our country. Often never knowing the outcome or back story, you just hope it all works out for the afflicted and the families involved.

When people talk about post-traumatic stress, they often think of the most extreme incidents, but the incidents that left the deepest memories for me were the ones where the utter sadness of the circumstances was never really resolved. This is who and what you will think about when as a retired cop you listen to the news and hear about crimes, accidents, and tragedies. Besides your obvious thoughts and prayers for the victims and their families, you think about the police, paramedics, and firefighters who responded, and the mechanics of the investigation or clean up after the incident. I do not know if you can call these things post-traumatic stress or just cumulative post-tragedy sadness.

As I was writing this, I realized how many stories there were to tell about people who died or nearly died alone, just from my experience. When you multiply for all the other first responders out there, it only compounds the post-tragedy sadness. I will drive by places in the city now and see a house or an address where I had been for a sudden death and still shudder from the memory of the sadness of the call. It is involuntary, and there is not really a lot you can do about it.

Experience helps, and at the same time costs. Depending on the individual, experience can also wear you down. So many questions and not many answers: Did anyone claim the body of the person who died alone? What happened to the house? Did the long-estranged family members come together in the end?

Just prior to my retirement presentation, one of the newly promoted sergeants told me a story of a call we were at together years before. She was a young constable just out of field training and working her first rotations on her own when she got dispatched to a sudden death. An elderly woman had passed away and her husband had discovered her and called it in.

She had arrived first, and knowing that she was still relatively new, I thought I would go and give her a hand until the patrol sergeant arrived. One of the first things a police officer arriving at a reported death has to do is confirm death. If the paramedics are there as well, they confirm the person is dead. The next thing the officer has to do is eliminate foul play. Then they have to do what they can to make the survivors as comfortable as possible, all the while still doing their job.

When I got to her call, I quickly took in as much as I could and was satisfied by the grieving husband's demeanour and the repose of his deceased wife. This was not at all suspicious. I did not remember all the details until she started telling me the story. I told the husband that I was sorry for his loss and asked him how long they had been married. When he replied sixty years, all I could do was put my arms around him and give him a hug. In my mind, his impending loneliness and sense of loss would be overwhelming. The sergeant finished her story by telling me the simple gesture of hugging someone in pain helped shape the police officer she wanted to become. I was glad to have been a part of it.

I talked a lot about empathy and compassion with the men and women I worked with. Sometimes they told me stories of calls they had been at where I was not involved, and I was in awe of their abilities to relate to people in crisis. One officer was at a call of a sudden death just before Christmas a couple of years ago, again an elderly couple living on their own. When the woman's husband would not wake up, she called the paramedics. The paramedics responded, found the husband dead, and called the police. The officers who arrived in short order established that there was nothing suspicious at all about the death and got to work trying to find someone to care for the wife. The wife may have had the onset of dementia and refused to believe her husband had died. She kept telling the officer, "He just won't wake up, why he won't wake up?" The way the officer told me the story made me realize that the sadness of the call affected her. The picture she painted telling the story stuck in my head for a long time afterwards. These types of calls are the ones that stay with you for the longest time and can weigh you down even if you had not thought they would, but they are the kind most police never talk about.

I think almost all of us have at one time or another laughed at a commercial where an elderly person has fallen and can't get up. We laugh with the arrogance of youth, probably because we are uncomfortable with idea that it can happen. It happens much more frequently than people think. Paramedics, firefighters, and police have all been to these types of calls and will continue to as our population ages.

The winters here in Saskatchewan and for most of Canada influence just about everything we do, but we tend to try to endure them as if the season were not happening. We are just in a holding pattern until the weather gets better. The cold and snow make for uniquely Canadian challenges for the police. Seniors living alone are especially vulnerable and at risk. Police and paramedics are often the first contact when there is a concern for their well-being.

A couple of years ago, Saskatoon was hit by one of the worst blizzards in recent memory. The storm literally shut the city down, except of course people who had gone to school or work before the full fury of the storm hit. Those people still had to get home. Transit buses were getting stuck, private vehicles were being abandoned on the roadways, and of course emergency services were being overwhelmed by calls for service. Police vehicles were virtually useless in these conditions and were getting stuck almost every time they stopped at a call.

Two constables responded to call from the neighbours of

an elderly man who had not been seen for several days. I knew from experience how these types of calls usually ended and began the arduous drive in my two-wheel-drive patrol car through the snow. The officers arrived at the address and saw mail was piling up in the mailbox. The walkways appeared not to have been shovelled in a while, wild blizzard notwithstanding. The windows of the home were frosted over. The officers questioned the neighbours, and on the surface it appeared that the occupant was a bit of a loner and perhaps had just gone away. The officers knocked on the doors and received no answer. The constables had at that point satisfied all the requirements of officers attending these types of calls. There was nothing to indicate anything was amiss. But between the two of them, they were not satisfied, so they climbed up to a window and scraped away the frost. Inside, they saw a man lying on the floor. They quickly relayed the information to Communications. I was still making my way to the call, so I radioed them to do whatever they had to do to get into the house.

Miraculously, the man was alive—barely, but alive. I got there and saw the damaged door and was impressed with extra effort the officers had put in at this call. Paramedics arrived, and the man was evacuated to the hospital. He had been lying on the floor for at least three days. We searched the house for any emergency contact information and could not find anything. We searched further and found some letters from Eastern Europe. They were quite dated and did not really help a lot. Eventually, we found some church documents, which led us to the church he attended. I contacted the father of the parish and asked if he could help us find who the man's relatives were. He went to work and eventually found a sister in the man's old country. I relayed the information to the hospital.

I wrote up the constables for a commendation for going above and beyond what was required, especially during a blizzard with many calls needing attendance. The official response was that it was their job and a commendation was not warranted. I do not know how long the man lived afterward, but I did know that because of the actions of those officers, he did not die alone.

One day shift in 2004, a call came in from an apartment manager in downtown Saskatoon. An elderly woman had not been seen for a couple of days and the neighbours were concerned. The paramedics, another constable, and I arrived at the same time. The building manager explained the circumstances and provided the pass key. I wish I could say differently, but most of these calls end sadly with a person found alone and deceased. I used the key to open the door and found the door chain was in place. These chains provide very little security, and you are better off with a deadbolt. I put my shoulder into the door and the chain gave way. I was immediately struck by a powerful smell, almost ammonia-like. The smell only reinforced my belief that the occupant had passed away. The apartment was neat and clean with no signs of a disturbance. These calls are never routine, and your heart pounds until you find the person. As I approached the bedroom, I could see the woman's feet. She was lying on the floor between the bed and the window. I approached to confirm what I suspected when suddenly she said in a forceful and fearful voice, "Who is there?"

I jumped back, startled and happy at the same time. It was the biggest shot of adrenaline I had had for a long time. I hastily yelled for the paramedics, who quickly established that the woman had fallen a couple of days before. Though she was severely dehydrated, she was going to survive. As they evacuated her, I could barely stop shaking, she had surprised me so much. The story had a good ending at least, but the constable who was with me told me she had never seen me so rattled in all the years we had worked together.

I took away a life lesson from all of these incidents, and I would pass it on whenever I could. No matter what kind of family dispute arises, always mend your fences. Regretting the loss of contact with your family members after they have passed is just unrelieved pain. Some people will do their best to drive you away, and others' deteriorating mental health will make hard for you to maintain a relationship. But no person should ever have to lie on a floor for days or die alone because of an unresolved family or mental-health issue.

No one, no matter what your occupation is, knows his or her capacity for dealing with tragedy and trauma. A cluster of suicides in 2014 and 2015 of first responders and soldiers underscores the need for leadership. Leadership in emergency services can get so caught up in responding and reacting to the calls for service that they forget that the service comes with a price tag to the mental health of those providing it. Leadership can be so simple sometimes, and why it seems so challenging to some is baffling to me: a simple "Are you all right?", and if the answer is no, follow it with "What do you need?" It is a common-sense investment in your people. Ensure your people have all the resources they need to do the job that needs to be done, then be sure to check on the people who did it.

Personally, I am a lot better than I was. Writing helped. Talking about things always helps. No blame assigned to anyone involved in first response—we learn as we go.

30

POST POLICE

IT IS INEVITABLE that criminals, either retired, incarcerated, or active, either read my first book or will read this one. Some will read it to see if they are in it. Some will read it to see if any police tactics are revealed. Either way, if they are reading, I get a chance to say a few things free of the tension and the suspicion of face-to-face contact. If I could say a few things to possibly make a person step away from crime, what would they be? Like a top-10 list, here is what I always wanted tell criminals.

1. *Although they may gain notoriety, there are no criminals who are held in high esteem by the rest of the world. From my experience, most criminals are alone when they die, their bodies and spirits broken. You should choose a different path.*

2. *A lot of crime is about self-hate. Quit hating yourself and projecting that hate onto others with your crimes.*

3. *Drugs—getting high, getting other people high, and getting wasted—is the cancer of all cancers. Believing that it is relieving you of your problems is the lie that will kill you fast.*

4. *The pain you cause to your victims, your family, and your community is hard to forgive and forget. Especially by you, once you realize the damage you caused by embracing crime.*

5. *Fellow criminals, especially when money is at stake, will never have your back.*

6. *The police, except in very rare cases, are better trained and equipped than you are.*

7. *If you have not been to real prison yet, imagine being locked into a featureless room for years, with maybe an hour or two a day where you get to see the rest of the house, which is full of people who do not love or value you.*

8. *Think of the person you would never want to see you commit a crime whenever you think you are going to commit one.*

9. *If you are criminal, you can make the personal choice to stop. You will have enough fence-mending to do in the first little while to keep you busy.*

10. *There are a lot of people who will help you. As a police officer, I valued victims over you, but I always believed that on some level, everyone had something good to offer. You have to help yourself first, though, before people will believe in you.*

In April 2014, I went to a concert with my oldest son. He had bought tickets to a British heavy metal band I had listened to since I was fourteen years old called Black Sabbath. The band was playing at Saskatoon's largest entertainment venue. I had been retired from policing for six months at this point, and I had had relatively few incidents related to my prior employment up to this point. I thought that the concert would be a good test of my ability to move around in the community where I had arrested so many people. Not everyone who listens to heavy metal bands is law-abiding or willing to put things behind them.

We had gotten a beer and were on the concourse heading to our seats when I saw two men I had arrested years before. Both biker types, they recognized me right away and started in my direction. I was making a plan for which one to take out first if it came to it when the bigger of the two thrust out a hand and said, "Congratulations on your retirement. Glad you are gone, but good job."

The smaller guy said, "You were a prick, but you were always fair." Both of them then added for emphasis, "We're glad you're gone."

I did not know what to say besides thanks, and I raised a cup to them and we went to find our seats. Several other people I had dealt with echoed the same sentiments throughout the course of the show, and while I never totally relaxed, I enjoyed the performance. It was an affirmation for me of a policing style I had tried to live by. If you want to leave a mark, this might as well be the one you leave as a street cop: firm but fair.

I was presented with this blanket after a presentation in Prince Albert, Saskatchewan, after my retirement. I was humbled and honoured. *Source:* Ron Merasty, Prince Albert

BIOGRAPHY

Source: Eagleclaw Thom, Regina

ERNIE LOUTTIT WAS BORN in Northern Ontario and is a member of the Missanabie Cree First Nation. He began his career with the Canadian Armed Forces at seventeen years of age, and in 1987 became only the third Native person hired by the Saskatoon Police Service. He spent his entire police career on the west side of Saskatoon, where he became known as Indian Ernie. His first book, *Indian Ernie: Perspectives on Policing and Leadership*, is based on those years on the streets.

Since retiring from the Saskatoon Police Service in October 2013, Ernie's first book has led him to a new career in motivational and public speaking, as well as writing. While these opportunities are not as dangerous as being a police officer, he finds them just as exciting and rewarding and is thankful for them. He lives in Saskatoon with his wife Christine and their four grown children.